God is out

> *"This above all : to thine own self be true*
> *and thus it must follow*
> *as night the day;*
> *thou canst not then be false to any man"*
> — **William Shakespeare**

Journeys into the Soul trilogy

Book 1 Follow Your Heart - The journey
   A story of Miracles, Magic and one man's adventure.

Book 2 Drops of Rain and Grains of Sand – The understandings

Book 3 God is out, please take a seat in the waiting room
         The lessons

God is out

Please take a seat in the waiting room

Michael Fleming/Brahmacharya Baba

Published by Michaels Rainbow

Copyright © 2018
by Michael Fleming/Brahmacharya Baba
All rights reserved.

ISBN: 978-0-9910130-1-2

Printed in the United States of America

ACKNOWLEDGMENTS

Gregory Zabilski for the back cover portrait of me

Cover photography by Michael Fleming

Man Dead? Then God is slain.
Ray Bradbury 1977

Edited by Steve Hoffmann who always pulls out the best in me.
and Sidney Chriqui who understands and supports my work.

I'd like to thank Claire Sarradet and Soumitra Basu
for helping me to know that most people
do not understand what I understand.
I have re-written the book with this in mind.

A few notes from friends
who have previewed my book:

Rock the world with it Michael.
       Ronni Sanlo, Sequim, Washington

My Dearest Brahmacharya Baba, I have never read such writing in my life. I love you very much.
(Referring to Who AM I).
 Ma Jaya Sati Bhagavati, Sebastian, Florida (Deceased)

Dedicated to that which is called, God

To Seth,

Niel Donald Walsh's God

Og Mandingo's friend the Ragpickers God

and my own god/God

Also to the various expressions of god/God that we all experience in one way or another, whether we realize it or not, and - - well, read on.

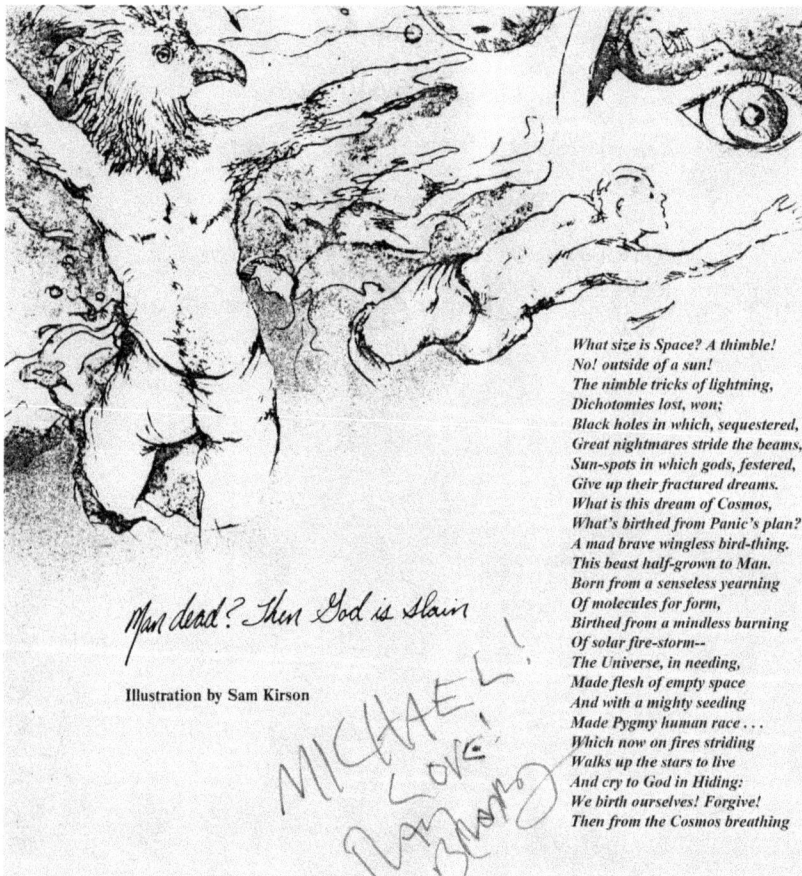

What size is Space? A thimble!
No! outside of a sun!
The nimble tricks of lightning,
Dichotomies lost, won;
Black holes in which, sequestered,
Great nightmares stride the beams,
Sun-spots in which gods, festered,
Give up their fractured dreams.
What is this dream of Cosmos,
What's birthed from Panic's plan?
A mad brave wingless bird-thing.
This beast half-grown to Man.
Born from a senseless yearning
Of molecules for form,
Birthed from a mindless burning
Of solar fire-storm--
The Universe, in needing,
Made flesh of empty space
And with a mighty seeding
Made Pygmy human race . . .
Which now on fires striding
Walks up the stars to live
And cry to God in Hiding:
We birth ourselves! Forgive!
Then from the Cosmos breathing

Man dead? Then God is slain

Illustration by Sam Kirson

An answering word from Him:
"No, dwarf-child, self bequeating
I birthed you as a whim.
I laughed you from the darkness
I dropped you as a joke,
But, strange small fragile creature,
You fell but never broke!
And now I see you laughing
As if the joke were yours;
Perhaps we made each other
In some wild common cause.
So let us share a hubris
Take common flesh as bread,
And drink each other's laughter,
Fall from each other's bed.
But careful, darling monster,
Your laugh might crack your soul,
Wha't yours is mine, remember--
We, separate, are Whole."
God laughs and Man gives answer,
Man laughs and God responds,
Then off they glide on rafters
Of stars like skating-ponds.
And which is God or Human
Let God now truly say:

"We fly much like each other,
We walk a common clay.
I dreamed Man into being
He dreams Me now to stay--
Twin mirror selves of seeing,
We live Forever's Day.
If Man should die I'd blindly
Rebirth that beast again:
I cannot live without him.
Man dead? then God is slain.
My Universe needs seeing,
Tha's Man's eternal task;
What is the use of being
If God is but a mask?"
So Man and God, conjoining,
Are One, uncelibate,
And spawn the Cosmic rives,
In billions celebrate.
No Ending or Beginning.
No crease, stich, fold or seam;
Where God leaves off, Man's starting
To recompense the dream.
Behold! the Mystery stirring . . .
Here come the human moles!
To rise behing God's masking
And peek out from the holes.

By Ray Bradbury

God is out -
Please take a seat in the waiting room.

Part 1   Journeys of self discovery in two short stories

      Helmuth and the enchanted forest
Helmuth defies tradition and leaves home looking for himself

      The Placement
Angela dies and wonders why she has not been judged.

Part 2   You and your own connection with god/God

      Who Am I?

Part 3   Combined works

          Truth – How to know it.
          Creation – How we create our own world.
          Judgement – Is there such a thing?
          Death – What happens when we die?
          god/God – You and your own relationship
              with All That Is

   3   Let God now truly say.

      The God Memorandum
      The New Gospel

> Q: Where is God?
> A: He is out.
> Q: When will he return?
> A: When you no longer have to ask.

When you hear the word, "*God*," what comes to mind?
People picture many differing things; a burning bush for some,
God as depicted in a painting or a statue.
A loud booming voice coming from a billowy cloud?
Or on a man on a giant throne perhaps who will punish or reward
   you as Michelangelo depicted and religions teach about?
Some believe there is no god at all.

What do you think will happen when you die?
Again, people think many different things:
Some think there will be nothing more and it will all just be over
while others picture a Utopian heaven of endless bliss, or burning
   hell fires and eternal pain.
- - Still others will be met by many virgins.

Is there a pending "judgement" of the life just passed?
The good and bad you have done or not done?
How you have dealt with the problems, gifts and situations
this life has presented to you?
- - Will this be judged?

Again, many quake inside fearing retribution for the sins they have committed while others piously expect to be ushered into high places and face that which you call God, Allah or some other name for *The Supreme Being*?

What do you think would happen if "He" were out?
Or what if you could have your own personal relationship with
God? - - What if you already have it?

This book is about you and your personal relationship
with that which is called, God

MF/BB

Part 1

Journeys of self discovery

Setting the mood for what follows with two short stories

Helmuth and the enchanted forest

Helmuth lives in an isolated village in the middle of an enchanted forest. He lives his life as his fathers and forefathers before him have done and follows the beliefs that have been passed down from generation to generation until...

Who among us is not afflicted by this feeling? I say, 'afflicted' because following what has been taught without question can create severe limitations to your personal growth.

This is a story about each of us if we have the courage to become that which we are.

We begin part 1 with one who could be you in many ways; Helmuth believes what he has been told.

But what of his own feelings? Is that not a direction as well?

God is out

Helmuth turned the last corner and ran for his home. The rain falling on the ancient cobblestone lane echoed the sound of his footsteps in the night. Now he was safely inside, the wooden door protectively closed and bolted, - - he was home. He pushed back against the door as if it could bar the thoughts from racing through his mind. It was quiet inside.

He tried to get his emotions under control. In his mind he traveled back to the Inn where the stranger had been telling his tales. Helmuth and his friends usually met at *The Sheltered Inn* to share a mug of ale at night and tell each other the doings of the day and any gossip that might have come their way. A fire burning nearby warmed the area where friends could sit and talk while quenching their thirst. This night as Helmuth was finishing his ale and ready to go, the leave-takings were cut short as a tall stranger entered the inn. Everyone stopped what they were doing and more than a few tankards were paused hovering in the air.

Travelers were rare in Kumar and all eyes were on the newcomer.
Old Tam Bell, the hefty innkeeper, came out from the back room wiping sweat from his eyes and brushing crumbs from his apron.
He waved to the young men to mind their own business, then led the stranger to the bar and asked after his needs. What the man wanted was a room for the night, a mug of ale and something to eat. Tam poured a mug for the stranger and bade him sit in front of the fire.
He shooed Helmuth's friend Mat from the softest chair and soon Ma Bell was serving the stranger a large bowl of her famous soup and some fresh hot bread.

Helmuth and his friends tried not to watch as the stranger dunked his bread in the soup and ate with relish, or when he took a great drink from the tankard. After drinking deep and wiping foam from his mustache he turned to Old Tam and gave such a smack of his lips that it seemed everyone in the inn could taste it. It was Old Tams best batch of ale, the one he served only on special occasions.

Soon the curious young men asked the stranger his name and where he was from. He looked at them for a moment then said his name was Admagil; "Admagil Watt; Admagil," he told them, means *One who journeys afar.* But," he said rather pointedly, "my name changes where ever I go as journeying is looked upon very differently in different places."

Helmuth, with big eyes looked at his friends--they were all shuddering at the very thought of "different places and journeyings." Aside from Sandborough on the other side of the great forest few even dared think there might be "other places" out there somewhere let alone actually going farther than the Sandborough market square; such thinking simply wasn't done in Kumar and few even wanted to go as far as that.

"As to where I am from," he continued with a twinkle in his eyes, "you could say that I am from everywhere and nowhere."

Few strangers chanced into Kumar and when someone did, they almost always came from Sandborough. So as far as "everywhere and nowhere," was concerned, everyone just shook their heads in wonderment.

Spurred on by another tankard of ale paid for by Helmuth and his friends, the stranger wiped bits of food from his beard, took a long drink, wrinkled his lined face and narrowed his eyes as if he was looking into the distance, then began telling tales of far away places.

Admagil Watt had a strong body; his face was wrinkled; not from age but probably from experience, with skin darkened by the sun. He wore a rough spun shirt like the villagers, and loose trousers that were so travel worn that Helmuth had to squint to guess at their original rusty color. His long hair was neatly gathered in back and tied with a length of cloth. He had a mustache and a short beard that went from ear to ear, but one could tell even from a distance that he was in need of a shave.

The young men bought several tankards of ale for the strange man to keep him telling his stories, but Watt seemed to delight in the telling of stories drink or not. They fidgeted back and forth on the wooden benches with fascination as his tales unfolded. Old Tam leaned over the bar and listened, as did the others who quietly and slowly nibbled their meals. Even Ma Bell found excuses to linger outside her kitchen, wiping and cleaning tables that had no need of it. Light from the fire flickered off the walls and faces as he told of places that lay across great bodies of water, called oceans; even larger than Lake Kumar on the outskirts of the village.

The lads exchanged knowing smiles upon hearing this, - Lake Kumar is the biggest body of water that the Kumarians have ever seen or heard of. Young and old alike enjoy going there to fish and swim on sunny days away from work and chores. The lake is so large it can take a whole day just to paddle across and back. No one stays on the far side for long though, nor do they venture into the river that it comes from and later on goes back into the forest.

Watt's eyes darted around the small gathering as he told his tales; where he found fear his eyes continued on, for he was looking for faces that were brightening with interest. His eyes rested on Helmuth. As he continued to describe wondrous places, Helmuth alone had a look of wondering in addition to the looks of fear that everyone else showed.

Warmed to his task and with a conspiratorial smile Watt said that to cross these great bodies of water, huge boats were needed; not the small boats that were used in Kumar but boats that were bigger even than the entire Sheltered Inn itself. Raised eyes and winking back and forth between the lads confirmed that they all wondered at the truth of these *oceans and boats and things.*

Watt told of fish in these waters that were so large they could swallow an entire person, and others with legs that could hold a man while devouring him. Some of the women scattered around brought their hands to their mouths in horror, Ma Bell grabbed her apron to her chin and shuddered and even the boys were shaken by the thought.

Admagil saw the looks of panic and smiled. "Yes," he said, "the world outside can be a shocking and dangerous place, but a wondrous place as well." He told of great towns called cities across those waters; - - cities even larger than Sandborough itself! He pictured animals that were enormous and even stranger than any the kumarians could ever imagine. Some with horns that were longer than his outstretched arms, others with necks as long as the common room was tall, and so flexible they could wrap them around their whole bodies! Some animals were huge while others were tiny. Some smooth skinned, furry, scaled or covered with a shell. When he described birds with feathers, long and more colorful than Old Mama Yuan's flower garden or small timid fat and furry animals that would trip and roll over themselves trying to get away and hide from prying eyes, everyone smiled with the pictured thoughts. Of course none of those gathered around the traveller believed these stories, nor had they ever been challenged with such thoughts before, and they tended to think of them as "Fairy tales."

Both Kumar and Sandborough were only small villages according to Watt. Soon the young men started to believe that perhaps Admagil Watt had indeed come from "Everywhere and Nowhere.

As they listened; their eyes grew large and filled with wonderment - - or squinted in dis-belief as the man unfolded his stories. They would be still there, drinking ale, warming themselves in front of the slowly burning fire and listening to the strangers tales if Old Tam had not shooed them out, telling them that he had to clean and close the inn and that Admagil Watt needed to be shown to his bed.

Helmuth felt troubled after listening to the man, for sometimes Watt had looked fixedly in his eyes as he spoke. *Why,* he wondered, *did the stories (and his eyes) leave him so unsettled?*

Parting from his friends, he began to wend his way home. His pace, slow at first, had quickened until he was running.

Now he was safely inside and could think the thoughts that had driven him hurrying for his home and safety–*but safety from what?* It wasn't the strange animals, birds, the great waters or large cities that filled Helmuth's mind as he leaned against the door, it was the last story Watt told that had his heart pounding.

"There is a very special place hidden deep within the Jochkum forest itself," Admagil had begun the story; "a place that few ever dare look for, non the less find, - because in order to find it they must leave the safety of the pathway. Only the brave make the attempt and only those that go with a longing for deepest truth can find it." Watt described a place of profound revelation where all things are known, all things are shared and deepest love is found. "A place of such truth and light," he continued, "that only the gods stay there for long and even the sun goes there to rest after it has left the sky and caused night to come.

The look on his face and the glow from his eyes as he recounted the tale convinced Helmuth that this amazing place really did exist along with his other stories. Helmuth was convinced that the stranger had actually left the pathway, there was no longer any doubt about it.

While Kumarians enjoy tales told by occasional passers by, the stories Watt spun were so outlandish that most did not believe them and some even laughed. But slowly the stories seemed to find a place within Helmuth's mind and he begun to feel a longing to see the places that Watt described. While the very thought of leaving the pathway filled him with fright, his descriptions left him–fear and all, with a burning desire to do just that. It was a place not so far from home, yet in so many ways even farther away than the great cities Watt had described in his tales. His mind had conjured wonderful images as the stranger spoke. The more he heard, the more the longed to see these places, especially this place of truth.

Of course he wouldn't really try to go because to find it he would have to leave the pathway–this he could not do. However the words seemed to pull at him, and presently he began to wonder if it might just be possible to go through the forest and leave the pathway after all. He laughed at himself for thinking such thoughts–but he kept thinking of them all the same. Like fishing hooks the words pulled at him–pushed him and dared him. He tried to quell the longing; this was unthinkable. How could he do such a thing? Yet, something inside would not be gainsaid and the thoughts grew in his mind with each spoken word.

The majority of the villagers never left Kumar at all, but Helmuth had gone through the forest when as a young boy his Father had taken him to the great market at Sandborough; "Sandborough, The City of the seven gates;" but of course they had not left the pathway. "*Seven gates!*" For the first time Helmuth wondered just what 'seven gates' implied; other ways out perhaps? *Where might those gates lead?* Large villages called cities and great bodies of water came to mind.

At this point, It is important to know something of the setting and background of Kumar and the people who lived there. Kumar was the only village that lay within the vast forest called Jochkum. I use the term, "was," in relation to Kumar because though it still *is*, it has changed and is no longer as I have written.

The forest was enchanted, everyone in the village knew this. Travelers who left the pathway would be swallowed up by the trees and shrubbrush, most never to be seen again. But some did come back, though they came back "changed," soon left, and were never seen again. Thus it was that few of the townspeople ever left the village. Few had found the need and fewer still were able to find the courage to do it.

There are many stories of how Kumar came to be, so deep within the forest. Some say that the desire to stay among their own kind within their own village had been so strong that their very needs and desires; their own "Kumari" way of life itself had created the forest and the enchantment that went with it.

But Kumar is old beyond time and its true origins are unknown. The Kumaris are steeped in tradition and live their lives much the same as their parents and their parents, parents before them. Little that is considered new, ever finds its way into Kumar. They have a self sustaining way of life, isolated with little to cause adventure, trouble or problems--and the people like it just that way.

When a baby is born in Kumar, it is given a cup made jointly by close friends and relatives of the family. (Perhaps a jar or flask would be the better word for it is sealed with a lid). The flasks will be carried continually and prized above all things. They are always kept close and seldom removed; for doing so leaves behind a feeling of loss. As years pass, the flasks fills ever so slowly at first; with a colorless liquid that changes both in color and in clarity as a person grows older. Soon every person has a different colored liquid for all to see *as the flasks are always visible*.

No one knows exactly what this liquid is; where it comes from, or what it means, yet the flask can be seen to fill a bit when tears flow or love is shared. Some believe the liquid is formed from the tears inside that people hold back instead of let fall. There are many other ideas about the liquid, but for the most part the people simply don't speak about it nor wonder too much about what it really is. The only thing that everyone agrees with is that the liquid in the flask is always changing.

It is also important to know something of Helmuth, of whom this story is told; Helmuth has always been a rebel, a beloved rebel loving from his heart. He questioned the elders; more, he questioned their answers, searching out the scrolls told him the truth; often the elders were wrong. Helmuth was generous to a fault, perhaps this is why he is called a 'beloved' rebel. Once he even tried to share liquid from his flask but Curate Bevcon stormed at him that he should never try to do that again. He never gave up the desire to share this wondrous liquid though, for he felt that it was the very essence of himself. *Was he alone in wanting to share this essence? One must ask.*

Now he could feel the rough wooden door pressed against his back helping him to return from his reverie.

And so it is that we find Helmuth on the eve of tomorrow; the tomorrow that is spoken of and found in books but rarely ever experienced.
    Even in his sleep he tried to think that tomorrow would be a day like any other, yet another part of him echoed back that this was not true; in his head the thoughts of leaving were growing stronger.
    As he went to his bed he was unsure what the morning would bring, but on the morrow, Helmuth will leave his home, friends and family, perhaps even his very life—to begin a quest; though he does not know what that quest is, drawn by a force that he does not understand yet cannot deny.
    Sleep did not come easy and minutes became endless hours before slumber came at last.
    Awakening with the first rays of the sun, he knew that he was going to leave. Even his dreams had supported this decision; sketchy dreams of walking down a beautiful pathway with light streaming onto his cheeks. In his dreams he had even been singing to himself as he walked.
    Upon wakening, he made a quick meal of boiled grains and pieces of mixed dried fruit. With shock he realized that he was even eager to begin this adventure. How, he wondered, could he be looking forward to leaving his home and his life? It simply wasn't done. Now he just wanted to get his firstmeal finished so he could leave. He was so anxious he was actually watching the water, willing it to heat and feeling as if it would never come to a boil. He gathered some food and water into an old cloth bag. A blanket as well he stuffed inside. That was all he could think of to take. He wasn't sure how long the journey would last but he did feel that it would not

take for long. He wrote a quick note to explain that he had left. He wasn't sure who would find the it but he knew that within a short time one of his friends or family would find it and be certain that he had gone off into the forest, and certain death.

He looked around his cottage wondering if he would still call it his home. As his eyes inspected his small house, he saw an old pot that he had found and brought home; he used it to hold, - just things. Some other items he noticed as well, and he wondered as he left his cottage and his belongings behind if they would be there for him when/if he returned, or if it would all just become things left behind, to be forgotten with the past. He had always kept his small cottage clean and neat, so now with his firstmeal finished, he cleaned up his dishes and placed them back on the shelf. Then with a pat to his pillow and a sweep with his hands to smooth out his bedding he was ready to leave.

Again he wondered if his home and his life would welcome him back to their comfort when/if, he might return. Strangely, the feeling that he might not return didn't really bother him, well, not too much. He took a staff, his bag and of course his flask and went outside to face whatever fate awaited him.

Oh yes, he will take the pathway through the forest to Sandborough, and the enchanted place that is drawing him on. More importantly, the pathway that leads out of Kumar and his very way of life. He does not know how to find the place, but Admagil had said that with a heart that was true, the way would be known. Somewhere deep within the forest, a special place is/was calling to him alone.

2

Helmuth closed the wooden door behind him. Just last night he had huddled on the other side of this very door—then the door was safety, a barrier shielding him and his life; now it was separating a life that had been lived from a future about to unfold with both his past and his future at hand.

As the latch snapped shut behind him he paused at the finality of the sound resonating through the morning stillness. Shutting the door behind him meant more to him now. He hadn't thought that he might be leaving for good until this moment. The thought caught

God is out

him as he became torn between the old and the new, the familiar and the unknown, that which *is* and that which can be.

What is this feeling drawing me to do this thing he wondered, it was like strings were pulling at him; st*rings or threads perhaps, but not ropes.*

He tried to think of it as just going off on an adventure even though the very thought brought feelings that were strange and scary in themselves; one did not "just go off on adventures," in Kumar.

His footsteps, timid at first, gained in momentum, as he walked away. But he did turn and look back for a moment at his cottage, it looked so comfortable and safe, - but also predictable and routine, maybe that's why he was being drawn into this 'adventure."

Helmuth lived almost as far away from the village as the farm fields; it was convenient for him to work his crops and at the same time gave him the privacy that he enjoyed. Cottages were spread farther apart out here; often with a field in between; all of them however, fronted on The Farther Road, named because it reached farthest from the village. The Flowing River sometimes crosses The Farther Road on it's way into town; it reaches through the fields, winds its way through the village green and back into the forest from which it comes.

Turning away from his home he walked toward the village and the forest which lay beyond. Excitement began to grow, he felt eager now that he was actually on his way. The possibilities seemed endless as he quit looking into the past and instead into a future that was unfolding with each step.

Walking down the path to the village he realized how different it was now. His mind moved quietly into the cottages as he passed, with memories of being inside them sharing with friends and family. He wondered what those inside would say if they knew he was passing by. He had grown up here, and small towns being as small towns are, he was more often than not related, - sometimes not to distantly, to most everyone else in the village.

While his footsteps didn't falter, his pace did slow down considerably when he finally came upon the village green; a grassy area with the Flowing River running through it. Around the green were spaced a few of the more important buildings in Kumar where ancient Rubbergum and smaller Fireleaf trees grew with shrubbrush interspersed between the buildings. A few large Rubbergum trees even grew within the green itself. While the Fireleaf trees were more beautiful because of the flowers that gave them their name, the Rubbergum trees were the favorite of all the people in Kumar. They were large and old with broad limbs that invited climbing and hiding. The Rubbergum trees had long ago been climbed, played in and told secrets to by almost everyone as they had grown.

Unlike people, trees do not forget secrets, because they become part of the rings of their yearly growth cycles.

On special occasions or for just sitting around chatting, the villagers would gathered on the green as evenings grew warmer and long. Sometimes the women would cook their favorite foods and there would be a village feast that everyone would talk about for weeks. Each woman would watch as people took of her food, then watch even more closely to see if eating it would bring a smile.

Sometimes Bertrim who helped at the church would trim the green; Curate Bevcon had long ago decided that it was the churches business to keep the green trimmed and neat because he *really* thought of the grass as the front lawn of the church; he kept this thought to himself, however.

The church stood at one end of the green; spire topped and whitewashed as if to illustrate purity. It was the only building that was not located among the trees, making it stand out, and as Curate Bevcon thought, added to the churches stature. For some, the church had a welcoming feeling but to Helmuth and his friends the spire resembled a hand that was raised in a gesture that said, "Halt or stop," probably because they were usually up to something of which Curate Bevcon wouldn't approve. None of them really believed in the precepts anyway and only attended church so that they could have an excuse to chat with the girls also so the ladies of the village wouldn't look at them with scorn.

The Curate was strict and usually found a treasure trove of activities in the village that would become fuel for the fires of his lecture on meeting day. He would rant and rave and when the young men finally escaped, (for that is the way they perceived it), they could usually feel sweat in the middle of their backs. They had long since decided that the only reason Bevcon was still the Curate was because people were afraid of him; fear they felt, kept him at his job, for he certainly wasn't well liked.

Next to the church stood the Sheltered inn. Made of rock and wooden timbers and sheltered on either side by large Rubbergum trees which is how it got its name; as rustic and cozy appearing as the church was pristine. Strange there was not a pathway between the church and the inn because it was more often that the Curate was found at the inn than it was that Tam Bell found himself inside of the church. Curate Bevcon liked to say it was Ma Bell's delicious cooking that brought him to the inn, but he never left without lifting several mugs of ale.

Helmuth thought of the many evenings spent at the inn drinking ale, laughing and joking with his friends, especially Thomos. Thomos was a mischievous sort, always up to something and Helmuth could never resist joining him in his next escapade. Helmuth was toughened by hard work, responsible and respected too, at least when he wasn't getting into trouble with *that Thomos boy*.

Old Mama Yuan's cottage was just, *up to the corner and to the right*. Not exactly in the center of Kumar so since she loved to visit with people she always kept a supply of her famous fresh baked cookies and some rather hard apple brandy handy to tempt any passers-by to stop and chat awhile.

Coming back to himself Helmuth turned away from the village and headed down the path that led to the gate and the forest beyond. At one time long ago the entire village had been enclosed by a wall as protection from whatever threat, real or imagined might issue from the forest.

The people of Kumar rested more securely at night knowing that the gate was securely locked. Helmuth felt a thrill of trepidation as he neared. He was gladdened however when he noticed that his friend Jachon was on duty. Jachon was one of the oldest and wisest men of Kumar, one of two gate keepers whose job was to warn of any trouble and make sure the gate was firmly locked at the setting of the sun then opened again each morning, and Jachon was a good friend.

He had worked at the gate ever since he was a young man and nothing that could be considered threatening had ever happened. What little happened was more interesting than dangerous; the arrival of the rare traveller or salesman who ventured the pathway or the still rarer villager that left. No danger and few travelers from the forest meant that Jachon's days were pretty languid. Mostly he napped or played biddly bong with anyone who was passing by had time to kill and wanted to play. Jachon lived in a small shack near the gate. Friendly with everyone in town, he also had opinions about most of the people he knew. Helmuth was happy to see him there, he really hadn't thought of encountering anyone when he left home but he should have remembered that there would be someone at the gate. He let Jachon believe that he was going to Sandborough but worried that the old man might suspect his intentions. If Jachon knew the plan of his young friend he gave no hint, but his eyes burned deep as he spoke of the dangers awaiting those who leave the pathway. Then he gave Helmuth a necklace. "This charm," he said placing it around his neck, "will help keep you safely upon the pathway." Helmuth accepted it and thanked his friend for his concern. Then he passed through the gate, and with a last look at the rising sun, entered the forest.

He remembered when his Da had taken him through the pathway; he had been young, happy and excited and enjoyed every minute of the trip; for him the journey was one of continuous adventure. When night fell they made a fire, got water from the stream running nearby, fixed a small meal, rolled up in their blankets and slept until morning when they continued on their way; all the way from Kumar to Sandborough of the seven gates and back again. *There was that Seven gates again.*

There was no, "The forest is enchanted," for him at that time, it was just that he got to go to the great market with his Father; holding Da's hand had helped of course. He knew of the enchantment now, not a good thing at best, and he could no longer hold his fathers hand for courage.

The pathway was well worn; not because so many people used it but because it had been there for a very long a time. It was always dim within the forest; the treetops mingled above expressing a feeling of protection but also leaving the impression that using the pathway was granted only by permission of the forest itself. Over time countless people had grown fearful of this feeling and turned back. While Helmuth *was* prepared for the feeling, a little more light might have helped. Slowly his eyes became used to the dimness and before he knew it the village and it's gate were left behind.

As he walked down the path he wondered about what he was leaving behind, he knew that he could return if he wanted but he had niggling feeling that he might not, or if he did he might come back "changed;" though he still didn't know in what way. *"Heck,"* he thought, *"I've already changed just by coming into the forest in the first place and I've barely left Kumar."* Spurred on by the message of Admagil Watt, he looked back to last night; *Was it only last night?* He could not tell if it was the words that Watt had spoken or the look in his eyes as he said them that lured him upon this unintended journey.

His eyes glazed in wonder at where he was and that he was there at all, and of course for the reason that he was there in the first place, what ever that reason was. How, he wondered, had he ended up on this journey.   Yet upon this pathway he was, and he now figured that he just might not be coming back.

3

All sounds were hushed within the forest, but softly, if one stopped to listen, birds could be heard gently chirping. Most didn't take note and only felt confined by the closeness of the trees. Only a small number actually ventured upon the Forest Road anyway, but few could walk it without being affected in one way or another.

It was called *The Forest Road* by everyone, although it was far from being a road; a narrow pathway amongst the trees was the more accurate description. Some had reservations about the journey and what they might encounter along the way so they were usually tense and insecure; bearing their worries with their shoulders rounded down as protection from fearful imaginings as they walked, eyes focused at their feet they saw nothing but oppressive trees guarding and limiting them, as a result their travel was seldom pleasant and usually not repeated.

There were those who stood to gain by bringing special items to Mrs. Jonas's store and taking canned goods from her cellars for sale or exchange in Sandborough. They had no fears to limit them and no interest in the forest, for their eyes were focused on the profit to be made. Having made the journey several times they were not afraid of the supposed enchantment and merely hurried on their way. But to a very few; Admagil Watt, Helmuth, and a handful of others, the forest was a special place; a place to be acknowledged, respected and hopefully entered. As Helmuth walked down the path his eyes were continually searching for a way into the forest.

*The forest; a living thing, knew the feelings
of those passing within her.
She closed herself to most who took the pathway but was
considerably more accepting of those who
appreciated where they were.*

Almost shyly she allowed some leaves to part; showing only hints of what lay inside, but Helmuth was so absorbed looking for a way in he didn't notice the brief glimpses she revealed as he passed. "*If only he would slow down and take the time to look,*" she mused to herself. Yes, the forest is a female, for the male force of Helmuth had to be balanced - this the forest understood.

After what seemed like several days, Helmuth came upon Sandborough without having found a way off of the path. It was near closing time so he took a bed at an inn.

The morning found him retracing his steps, still determined to find a way. Nevertheless determination soon wore away as each step revealed the same endless barrier of trees which grew so close they blocked any attempt to enter the forest itself. At night he slept beside the pathway wrapped in his blanket—trying to sleep really, for he was becoming discouraged as days passed—*or was it long minutes* he wondered, for time was changed within the forest.

He was leaning against a tree munching on a small bit of biscuit. It was taking longer than he had thought and his food was running low. At first Helmuth had resisted even touching the trees but now he was comfortably leaning against one. This in itself was a small victory. Sitting in the peaceful quiet he heard himself grumbling as he ate. He realized that he had become upset and even angry—yes, angry was the correct word. Why had he allowed himself to become upset? Was he mad at the forest? That seemed to be a waste of energy. This wasn't right, he had to calm himself. He hadn't felt this way when he had begun the journey.

He remembered when he had walked the pathway with Da as a child, all the way to Sandborough and back again; he had been delighted with the adventure and wondered why so few people made the trip.

As it had happened,, his father had planted a large crop of ice peppers, they were not called "Ice" because of being grown in cold weather *but for the feeling that they imparted when eaten.* They were highly prized and didn't usually grow well in Kumar. But since the family liked them his Da had planted many hoping to get a few. The year had produced a crop in abundance. Almost all that he planted grew and flourished. Of course Mrs. Jonas had gushed over the crop and wanted to trade for it, but Da felt he could get better for it in Sandborough; thus Helmuth got to go through the forest to help push the cart.

He had been excited then but now he was discouraged. He knew there had to be a way in, for he still believed in Admagil Watt. *What*, he wondered *was he missing?* He really was discouraged, he felt a tear drop from his eyes and knew that he was beaten.

Then slowly he began to think about what had been happening as he walked the pathway; in his minds eye he saw himself walking the pathway for the past few days or whatever it was: Hunched forward and not searching with his eyes as he had done when he left Kumar. He began to wonder if it might be his own feelings making the forest react as it was—or was not reacting at all, more's the point —the forest was enchanted after all. Deep inside he realized that he wasn't really expecting to find a way off of the pathway any more. Could it be that his own expectations were keeping him locked away from the forest's heart? Maybe he had expected the forest to reach out and grab him. *If I continue this way I will not really look, keep missing what may be right there in front of me. Also, searching in anger is not the way.* He needed to calm himself, nothing would be gained by storming along. These were the thoughts that kept him company as he rolled out in his blanket to sleep beside the pathway.

No, she would not let him in if he were angry or agitated,
- - and she did not reach out and grab anyone,
no matter what people said about her.

Over and over he pondered his own part in creating what was (or was not) happening. With a resolve to continue with a positive attitude in the morning, he allowed sleep. He had dreams of many leaves caressing his body; of mosses that cushioned and moistened his feet, and tree limbs that lifted to allow him to pass, but these dreams he did not remember.

Darkness grew lighter as *shadow light* edged away the nighttime. Morning found him feeling more positive about his venture, anyway there was nothing to loose by being positive. Freed from the nights wonderings he watched his thoughts and moods as he folded his blanket and continued down the pathway to start his journey anew,

Helmuth had not slept to one side of the pathway truth be known, for the pathway was not really wide and there were few footfalls during the night.

Now walking the pathway with new feelings he even whistled as he walked.

Is he whistling at me? she thought.
For the forest, although enchanted; did not know everything.

No, actually Helmuth was whistling to himself as a reminder to maintain an optimistic attitude. Remembering how he felt as he left Kumar, he smiled; the smile spread though his body, happiness replaced the dark moods that had beset him and now he continued on his way with a different intent in his mind and in his stride. He walked slower now; checking out the trees and leaves as he passed, he saw that he had been wrong about the forest looking the same.
Now he noticed that each leaf was different from the others; different in size, shape and coloring, making different patterns within the trees. This made his journey so much more interesting and he began whistling another tune.

Now she could feel his pulse and formed an intimacy
with him:
Slowly branch by branch, she began to reveal herself
as he passed.

Though the pathway was dimly lit he began to notice small areas of brightness shining at the edge of his vision. Light coming from between some leaves suggested depth through the foliage   and he caught brief glimpses into the forest. What had looked like an impenetrable barrier was beginning to look not so unyielding at all.

Yes, she thought, He has seen me.
Along with the rest of the forest he was inside of her now.

Looking deeper, he saw dappled light coming through tangled trees shining in golden ribbons to the ground below. He noticed those depths of light and thought deeply about what he saw;

Timidly, for she did do this often,
she exposed more of herself.

A seed that had laid hidden beneath fallen boughs and leaves throughout the winter, was now illuminated by a ray of light. The seed shell had cracked and a root was reaching out to give strength to the plant that was to follow, at the same time a seedling was reaching toward the light

The trees grew the seed pods and released them to the ground. As winter approached, wilted leaves dropped to shelter the seeds protecting them from the winter to come. As spring comes again, light and warmth causes the seeds to reach out and grow.

The forests cycle of life was being enacted in such simple beauty that Helmuth became overwhelmed and his breath came in gasps with the wonder of what he saw.

When evening came he lay down to sleep. Still shaken by the depth of what he had seen he twisted back and forth upon the ground. As he turned he felt something slide across his chest - the charm Jachon had given him not so long ago, *or was it long ago?* he was no longer sure. "This charm will keep you safely upon the pathway," the old man had said. Jachon was a friend, and *yes*, the amulet was still hanging around his neck. *But we aren't going in the*

same direction he thought, so gently he laid the charm beside the pathway.
Somewhere deep within the forest the last few chirpings of a bird sifted through the trees and a restful sleep came easily now, along with a few fleeting dreams.

Morning came; the sun already shining in Kumar found it's way through the foliage to shine with different patterns on the ground and spread the daily gift of light. Released now from the well intended wishes of his friend he began to think better of his chances. So with renewed thoughts and vitality Helmuth continued on down the path. As he walked he sensed that the morning felt differently. He had only taken a few steps when he noticed a shadow being cast before of him outlining his own figure on the path - there was some kind of light coming from behind him. He paused for a moment then turned to see where it came from. A glow seemed to radiate from behind him where he has spent the night (and laid the charm aside).

He hesitated for a moment, unsure if he should continue or return to see what was shining. He had started out with such gusto that he was tempted to continue, but curiosity won him over and slowly he walked back the way he had come. The closer he came the more the light seemed to glow.   Coming upon the amulet he noticed that a leaf was laying beside it; the leaf was fresh, not withered as one would expect of a fallen leaf. Helmuth knew that fresh leaves rarely fall from trees. *Was this a message from the forest?* Drawing nearer he could see that the light was coming from between two trees that had grown together in such a way as to form a small archway which could not have been seen as one walked normally down the path. He peered into the opening and was astounded to see a pearlescent glow coming from the darkness within the forest—here was an opening and he only had to stoop a little to pass beyond.

Once within the forest the first thing that he noticed is that there was no longer a pathway to follow.

4

Helmuth had left the pathway completely behind and was now fully surrounded by the dense forest, there was no trail to be seen. If there was to be a way in it would have to be made by Helmuth himself. He took a tentative step into the woodland; the leaves themselves bent shyly out of his way. After a few steps he felt as if the trees and shrubs molded themselves to him as well. It was not an oppressive feeling at all, almost like swimming in a lake of leaves. There was nothing to be done except to move ahead. The plant life brushed him sensually as he walked deeper into the forest. He did not know where he was going because he couldn't see very far at all. While giving way to him the foliage was still profuse. Sometimes he could see or maybe just sense some of the pearl light that had drawn him and he would head in that direction. Other times he could not see any glow at all so he just kept heading on the same course. No matter whether he followed a glimmer of light or his own lead, the forest formed itself both in front and behind him so that he became the pathway itself. His very breath seemed to change the air surrounding him.

While the leaves and limbs made way for him, his staff kept getting caught in the undergrowth. He liked his staff but within the forest it was no longer useful and kept getting in the way so he decided to leave it behind. He leaned it against a crotch of an old Rubbergum tree which reminded him of his favorite tree back home—the one that knew all of his secrets. Then he picked up his bag and began to move deeper into the forest but he had to stop and reach around to loose the bag from where it had become tangled in some shrubbrush. He didn't need to look inside to know that there was no food or water left, nothing that could be of use to him now. So like his staff, he left that behind as well. Making his way through the forest was easier now.

After a time the closeness of the trees lessened and he came upon a clearing with tunnel like openings scattered around a circular space. Deeply within each one sat a person nooked in a small alcove of trees and brush. They were almost surrounded by plant life and could not see in any direction but straight in front of them

—that direction was toward the emerging Helmuth.

He could see them and they could see only him if only they cared to look--but they could not see each other. Each was engrossed in doing something totally different from the others, acting as if they existed alone. Maybe they didn't know if any of the others were there or not.

As he stepped into the clearing he felt the leaves take leave of him. He missed their touch; oddly enough he had become quite used to the contact with the forest.

He could see a light coming from one of the openings near him. There was an old woman sitting before a small fire that she kept smoldering with twigs. She sat erect and wore a shawl that covered most of her body. He approached her. "Do you know the way to the place of truth and the setting sun?" he asked.

She did not stop feeding her small fire but looked at him and told him to put his hand into the flame. Tentatively he reached his hand to the fire but he did not actually touch it and pulled his hand back. "Is it not the setting sun itself?" she inquired, "Can you not feel the heat and see its light; is this not the truth itself?" Helmuth felt that this was not what he was searching for so he bade the old lady good day.

Leaving her "cubby?" He went to the next tunneled opening and peeked inside; a skinny, wrinkled old man with a very long beard was contemplating a small pool of water. Like the woman with the fire he seemed neither surprised nor frightened by Helmuth. Drawing nearer he saw that the sun shining through a parting of the trees above was reflected in the pool.

"You must be very still or it will disappear," the old man said without looking up. "Every day it comes to the pool for a time but you must be patient, surely this is what you seek." Helmuth could see the sun shining above and that the man was too transfixed by the fragile image in front of him to look up and see the real thing. Perhaps the man had never looked up at the sun; he certainly hadn't looked at Helmuth to tell the truth, so with a sigh he moved on to another opening.

A lady wearing very colorful clothing sat with her hands encircling something glowing between her fingers. Helmuth eyed her and asked yet again about the place of the setting sun and truth.

God is out

Slowly she opened her fingers and revealed a small but rather bright firefly nestling between her hands. "Is it not the resting sun itself? she said, "Is it not all truth in one?" But Helmuth saw only the firefly and the firefly would soon die and the light would be gone, so He took his leave.

He continued in this way around the clearing, asking at each one of the place of truth and the resting sun. While each was devout, each in his mind were found wanting; nothing that was told or shown, expressed the place that Admagil Watt had described.

In this way Helmuth found that truth is a personal thing clothed in many forms and different for each. All of them seemed to be content, and he realized that he had to find his own way.

There were no openings from the clearing except for those which held those people in their respective nooks. But remembering the leaves and limbs that had caressed him, he edged back into the forest.

First one leaf bent aside, then some brush, even a limb, and then he was surrounded intimately by the forest. *How comforting it had been to be caressed in this way.* Uncertain but still committed, he began again to make his way deeper into the forest that was drawing him on; at least he hoped he was going deeper for aside from the bladed afternoon light there was nothing to follow and he couldn't get over feeling that he was getting lost.
He did not feel fear but it wasn't long before he realized that he had become discouraged again. So he stopped and took a few minutes to lift up his mood. Then he put a smile on his face, let it seep into his heart and mind and began to whistle a happy tune to help cheer himself up.

Forests do not smile as we do - even enchanted ones;
she was however - delighted.

After a while the foliage began to grow less abundant, there was more space between the plant life and it grew brighter.

Leaves quivered against his hand as he shifted a branch aside. Then the leaves were no longer brushing against his body. He missed the closeness but thought that just maybe he was coming at last upon his goal. Trees first, then limbs, lastly leaves themselves parted away, except for an old leatherleaf tree whose limbs formed an archway. *"Looks like the same one I used to climb,"* he thought.

Passing under the familiar feeling tree he entered a large oval open space not unlike the village green that he had grown up with; except that there were no other openings leading away. The clearing was carpeted by small leafy plants creating a green ground cover.

Lined around the clearing, trees reached out long limbs stretching into branches that splayed themselves apart like fingers. They were not reaching up but out; gradually rising then falling in a fluid motion as they reacted to both a gentle breeze and to the dew dropping from they're quivering leaves. Dew made the leaves sparkle as if they were dressed in thousands of diamonds with rainbows reflected from the sun finally let in. The sunlight let him see deep into the forest revealing plants and trees glimmering in a plethora of shades of green. It was the most beautiful sight he had ever seen. Perhaps this was the forest's heart. *How* He wondered, *did I ever decide to go looking for 'The Forest's heart'?*

A feeling of wonder began to grow within him--even awe. He had never felt that anything in particular deserved admiration before; even when Curate Bevcon preached at his best he had never conveyed a feeling such as this. He was almost overcome with the sense of wonderment; *could this be a Holy place?* he thought. He wasn't sure what to do next or how to act, but if this was a holy place he knew that he should do something; he just wasn't sure what that 'something' might be. He supposed maybe he could bow; so slowly, with timidity he let his hands reach down the sides of his breeches. He looked about in embarrassment as if someone might see him bowing to the forest. As he reached his hands farther down, bending at the waist. An energy seemed to come up from the ground, into his feet, up into his body and back through his outstretched arms; returning to the earth from which it came. The energy continued to flow in a cyclical pattern that made him think of the little seedling reaching toward the sun while at the same time delving into the earth—the life cycle of the forest. Seconds, minutes, days, years merged into one. Thus he bowed to the energy that was there before him, around him, within him now and leading him on.

Though he didn't notice it, the leaves surrounding the clearing were shivering; *He has seen me,* She trembled.

He raised his head and looked at the sun centered in a blue sky with happy clouds all around. It was so stunning he raised his hands to the sky.

> *Yes, she thought savoring the moment,*
> *you are another who will know.*

Slowly the light in the sky began lowering. Dark shadows that had grown from the base of the trees drew slowly back into the roots beneath the ground from whence they came. The sun seemed to be gently descending in front of him.

Then a male Jackdaw called from a neighboring tree a female chirped back, - - there was a fluttering of wings.

She did not feed upon the energy of those few who entered her, but she was indeed exhilarated when it happened.
She was excited In ways that only a forest can be excited.

Then Helmuth took a step into the clearing,

5

While the sun seemed infinite in size, heat and light, its vastness seemed to be within his grasp, the light while far too bright was not blinding, the heat was as gentle as a warm breeze; this was certainly the place Watt had described. As his eyes adjusted to the light he began to see that there was someone or something coming from the middle of the brightness; a luminous being emerging opposite him. There was a space between them, yet they were close enough to see each other clearly.

A man shape it was, but was it a man or was it some kind of spirit, Helmuth could not be sure. He radiated such beauty as Helmuth had never imagined, the setting sun gave his whole body a - - radiance.

Awe, fear and love at the same time filled his heart. This surely is a god he thought, but not at all like anything Curate Bevcon would have preached; this was a person of such magnificence that the word god just seemed to fit; or maybe spirit was the right word.

Finally he decided it didn't matter because he had just noticed the resemblance between himself and the other; His heart leaped to his throat as he saw the other was wearing a flask very like his own, however his flask shined with a glow radiating with the delicate colors of a rainbow.

Then Helmuth looked at his own flask; the liquid was murky and had no shine at all. He had never thought about it before because all the people in Kumar had similar liquid in their flasks. But now he saw how drab it really was.

He noticed that the other wore no clothing. He seemed a perfect being as he stood there in the shining light, relaxed, unashamed. Helmuth looked down at his dirty, travel worn clothing, he felt that to wear such begrimed garments would befoul this seemingly holy space. So Helmuth took off his jerkin and breeches, even his shoes he sat aside. He folded them into a pile. Then he straightened and took another step into the clearing. The other took a step as well.

"Helmuth, Helmuth." He did not have to turn around to see who was calling for he knew the voice; "Helmuth where are you?" The voice sounded from within the forest but he heard it from deep within his soul - accompanied by a faint smell of fresh baked apple pie.   He remembered the day that he and Thomos were passing by Old Mama Yuan's cottage. They smelled a fresh baked pie, It was sitting on a window seal where she had placed it to cool. Thomos was always a mischief maker and Helmuth couldn't resist joining him in most of his designs. They sneaked up to the window took the pie and ran to the edge of the forest. Then hiding behind a tree they laughed with each other as they wolfed down the pie. They were not so far away that they could miss hearing as she called though; "Helmuth, Helmuth, where are you?" Old Mama Yuan was calling to him. He peeked around the edge of the tree, could see that she was all smiles as she called. Mouths full of pie they could not, did not answer. Although Helmuth noticed that his pie didn't seem to taste as good any more.

The following day, was the day of his Coming of age.
Mama Yuan came to his parent's cottage with a sorrowful look on her face. She had come to wish Helmuth a happy Coming of age. Wringing her hands in her apron, she said that she had used the last of her summer apples to make a pie as a gift for him, but someone

had taken it as it sat cooling in her window so she had nothing to give. She felt so badly she was in tears. All she could do was give him a hug, told him that she would try to make it up to him somehow. Helmuth did not admit that he had taken the pie. He was so ashamed that he had hurt Mama Yuan, and all she was trying to do was to give it to him as a gift.

He wasn't sure why they had taken the pie; Mama Yuan was never stingy with her cookies or pies. They were not thieves It was just a mischievous prank. Now her echoed voice evoked again that shameful exploit. As years passed the memory had faded but like a sliver that lay festering beneath the skin it came back to him now with the cry; "Helmuth, Helmuth, where are you?"

Comparing his flask to the shining rainbow across from him he now wondered if the liquid in the flask could in some way be reflecting things done in the past. The people of Kumar would never have acknowledged it of course; In fact the people of Kumar never mentioned it at all. But what if his flask contained the shame that he had just re-lived; how could he offer this to the shining being he wondered—for he was mindful that deep inside, this was what he'd always wanted to do.

He saw the smile, the radiance, the rainbow glow and for the first time he was ashamed about what his flask might contain. With a shaking hand he lifted his flask to his mouth and drank. The taste was rancid, old, bitter and dank. He almost fell over from the impact on his stomach. It tasted horrible; still his drinking was deep, he knew that he could not spill it upon the ground; *"You must never spill it upon the ground."* Then he noticed that the other had drunk from his flask as well.

Their eyes met as they took another step toward one another. The other one then drew off his flask, offered it to Helmuth. 'Yes," this is what he wanted so he took another step, the other wanted the same as well.

The sun peeked between some limbs above him, he looked toward the light and noticed the beautiful puffy clouds lazing in the sky. He idly thought, "What a perfect day to go swimming." Unexpectedly he added, "Isn't it Nestor?" In his mind he saw the disappointed look appear on Nestor's face. He knew that Nestor was very much afraid of water and wanted to go riding instead but Nestor looked up to Helmuth and not wanting to loose his friendship, usually went along with his wishes.

Now he saw Nestor's face as he stepped timidly into the water. Helmuth splashed him, wanting to play. He saw the fear on his friends face as he tried to join in the fun with his hero. Laughing at him he splashed him more then dunked him. How could he have been so thoughtless?

This too, was a memory that Helmuth could not offer to the other, so instead of extending his flask, he drank again. The taste was once more almost overwhelming. Surely he thought, this had to be enough to cleanse the liquid. But another ray of sunlight escaped from the top of a surrounding tree and shined upon the adjoining leaves making them sparkle even more. The sight brought a smile to his heart as a scene found a place within his memories; "No!" He cried.

His face wrinkled, his eyes filled with tears. It had happened when Helmuth was about ten summers. He and Thomos had been messing around in some trees and came upon Park's old horse; Dob was grazing free in Park's field. Park was younger then, he wasn't called "Old Park" yet. Thomos smiled a conspiratorial smile, as usual Helmuth could not resist. It was a beautiful day, the boys had wandered far out from town, there weren't any others about to see, so they sneaked into the field and took a ride.

Old Dob didn't go very quickly any more but they were enjoying themselves just the same. Birds were singing and there was a gentle warm breeze.

Riding just outside of the forest Helmuth noticed that the sun had just peeked above some trees, the light was shining off of the leaves in star like sparkles. What a great morning it was. Then they heard voices coming up the cobbled road so they quickly rode back into the field, took the halter off of Dob then ran and hid among the trees. It hadn't occurred to either of them as they ran that they had forgotten to rope the gate. Later that night Dob had pushed against the gate, went off wondering in the fields near the forest and was never seen again. Dob wasn't good for much anymore but Park had had her since he was a colt. Dob always hurried up to nuzzle him whenever Park came into the field. He had always been shy and had few friends but Dob had always been there when he needed a friend, and friends they were.

The following day it was all over town that Old Dob was missing. Many of the villagers volunteered to help find the absent horse. Helmuth and Thomos joined in the search as well. "Someone must have let loose the rope on the gate," Helmuth heard someone say. His heart fell. They looked all day but couldn't find Old Dob. Finally they had to admit that he was gone.

Park was the last to give up the search. His face was filled with sorrow, the look on his face was one of despair for he had just lost his best friend. He looked older now. He put his hands deep into his pockets and walked away. It must have been then that everyone started calling him, "Old Park."

"But it was me," Helmuth cried to the forest, "Me and Thomos." Falling on his knees he bowed his head and wept. Old Park was a good man; now Helmuth realized how badly he had hurt the old man. So again he drank from his cup. Tears streaming down his cheeks as he drank the bitter memory. He did not notice but the other drank as well. Helmuth remembered other things and tears continued to fall; bitter memories of bitter times: An unkind word here, a slight there; they all added up buried within his flask. With each memory he drank, the other drank as well.

While his heart was breaking from these dark and forgotten memories, the sun continued to shine as the glory of the forest surrounded him. He drank until there was no liquid left, then he shook the flask and licked the edge to make sure that none of the vile liquid remained.

He had drunk it all and none was let to fall to the ground.
Helmuth still on his knees, could see the other drinking the last droplets as well.

He stood slowly upon wobbly legs and faced the man shining in front of him. The other was smiling with brightly shining eyes that seemed to pierce into Helmuth's very soul. It seemed as if he could see all things in those eyes.

Then Helmuth was smiling as well. As one they set their flask's upon the ground and met in an embrace. Helmuth felt from the touch, such love as he had never thought possible. Inside a fullness began to swell, filling Helmuth so that he thought he would burst.

The other threw up his empty flask. He caught it back.

A flush of rainbow light fell upon Helmuth making him feel as if each pore of his body were being cleansed. He caught his breath in exhilaration. The other was gone and he stood alone. It was time to leave. He picked up his empty flask, put it around his neck, found his clothing and dressed.

Turning to leave he wondered momentarily how to find the pathway. Then he spotted a small opening between two trees. As he approached, the leaves moved aside for him to pass. While they brushed him gently they were no longer quivering as before. The forest did not look so impenetrable any more; it looked just like any other forest; but an exceptionally beautiful forest it was.

The pathway appeared just around another tree, and Helmuth stepped through as if from one world to another. He set down on the pathway to rest. Glancing down he saw that his flask was full again; with a liquid that was clear and shined with a likeness of a rainbow.

And again, she was very pleased.

The Placement

Angela has unexpectedly died. Like most religious people she expected to be standing in front of some giant on a throne who was about to reign terror upon her. But here she was, in a very nice (not golden towers nice, but nice) home with friends and places to go.
    Angela was not satisfied though; she hadn't yet been judged. There was a Placement Office in town. No one talked about it of course, but what else could *Placement* be? Her mind seem to be nagging at her. While others ignore the Placement Office; Angela is drawn to it like a moth to a flame.

Angela felt a bead of sweat working its way through her antiperspirant deodorant. *Damn it,* she thought, *happens every time I come here.* Immediately her mind badgered her about the word "damn." She hadn't said it aloud of course, she had just thought it, but in the back of her mind she remembered Reverend Bevcon sometime saying, "Even your thoughts must be pure; evil in mind is the same as evil in body."

Calming her mind, putting a smile on her face and with a resolve not to swear again, she pulled open the huge ornately carved door leading into the Placement Office. It always unsettled her that the massive door opened easily each time. As the door closed behind her, she looked for the sign on the secretaries desk. Oh no, she thought, not again. The sign read,

GOD IS OUT -
PLEASE TAKE A SEAT IN THE WAITING ROOM.

The first time Angela had come to the office she had been overwhelmed with wonder; although the office appeared fairly small from the outside, inside it was enormous. A vast panorama unfolded in front of her; fluffy clouds floated in a deep blue sky and it seemed she could see well past the walls that should have been there. There were even rainbows hinting themselves among the clouds, and some birds fluttering about.

Stranger still was that there was a secretary sitting at a desk behind the sign but in front of the sky. Chairs lined up like in a waiting room but there was no one sitting in them.

Angela had only come to the office to look around - not to be 'placed', just sightseeing as it were, like in a museum or art gallery.

She giggled about the thought of being on tour; "*And on your left is cloud nine.*" Then she noticed the sign on the secretaries desk; "GOD IS OUT," it said, "PLEASE TAKE A SEAT IN THE WAITING ROOM."

The secretary was a pleasant, elderly lady who made Angela feel at ease. She told her that since the Office wasn't being used at the moment she was welcome to look around since HE was out. She thought it might be fun to have a look in the waiting room. What a wonderful room it was—well designed, understated and cozy.

Before long she was sitting on the fluffy couch. Opposite her was a huge, ornately carved golden mirror; It didn't really fit with the decor yet it seemed appropriate somehow. From where it hung on the opposite wall it was hard to miss because no matter where she sat she could see herself looking back. She patted her hair and decided she looked fine. Then she happened to focus on her eyes in the mirror; they actually seemed to be looking at her. Of course if one looks at themselves in a mirror and see their eyes they will be looking back, but now they seemed to actually be looking at her leaving her with a slightly uneasy feeling and she quickly looked away.

The room was comfortable and welcoming and since she was already there, she decided to wait for God even though it would also mean Placement.

After a few hours in the waiting room without anything happening, her mood changed; the allure began to wear thin and she became a bit grumpy. Even though she had only come for a *look around* she felt discouraged and snubbed: *You'd think working up the courage to face God and placement would count for something.* Finally, dejected and even with a touch of sadness she gave up and left.

Angela often wondered where she actually was after ending up here. It wasn't the heaven that she had pictured and it certainly wasn't hell, so where was she? Thinking about 'here' brought up another thought, H*ow long have I been here?* Time was funny in this place there weren't any clocks or calendars so it was difficult to keep track of time and days.

The visit to the Placement office had aroused a desire within her however; to be where she really belonged—and to see and meet God truth be known.

She had thought a lot about judgement since she got here, where ever *here* was and expected to find herself in front of a giant God with a flowing beard passing judgement on her. She was relieved that didn't seem to be what was going to happen; *but where were the pearly gates that everyone talked about?*

The routine of her life changed then; transformed both by her visit and by wondering about placement in the first place. No longer at peace with herself, she felt conflicted and pulled apart. The desire to stay where she was clashed with the irresistible pull of the office that tugged at her. Down deep Angela was thinking about going back to that dam - - n (*caught it*), office.

She was unsettled and aimless even. Her sleep was restless; not that she needed sleep of course, it was just a habit left over from the life just past.

It was not long before she found herself at the Placement Office for the second time.

Coming from her 'home' through the forest had been comforting, but now standing in front of the carved door Angela became aware that she was scared. While she had just been looking around the first time—this time she had come to be placed. She started to turn to away, but realized she would still be wondering where she belonged and she really did want to know. So she opened the door and went through the doorway, It seemed that the carvings appeared to be looking at her so she quickly closed the door behind her.

She was horrified to find that instead of a beautiful sky to greet her she was in a dungeon surrounded by darkness. There were chains, metal devices and blood. Red fires were burning in different places and she could hear strange gurgling sounds and moans coming from the gloom. Crying out with fear she turned and ran from the office.

Oddly enough the secretary and her desk sat in front of the horrors, and she caught a glimpse of the sign on the desk; God was still out.

Slamming the giant door behind her she collapsed shaken and shaking. Panting and in tears she leaned back against the door for protection. Taking a deep breath (which really wasn't a breath at all just the feeling of breathing), helped calm her down. The office and the dungeon were on the other side of the door and she was safely outside.

Forcing herself to relax she wiped the tears from her eyes and slowly began to calm down. Thinking that the worst was over she took another non-breath. Then with a start, she realized that the worst could't possibly be over; she still hadn't had her interview with God, nor had she been placed. Could this be why her friends hadn't come to be placed? *I can't go back there.* With the door as a barrier against the terror on the other side she could think clearly and firmly rejected any idea of going back again.

Before long she felt somewhat more stable and started to walk home. A pathway began to form in front of her as she walked. When she first got here it had been unnerving to see a path being created this way and it took several attempts before she could walk without her nerves being frayed. She remembered that it sometimes happened that way in dreams but this isn't dreaming at all, is *it?* After a while however, she had found that walking this way through the forest had a relaxing influence.
   This is the way it is here—you get used to it.
   Wherever she wanted to go, a way would be made, but she did have to concentrate a bit else she didn't know where she would end up, and there had been some surprising results from just walking without thinking about it. The path could be long or short depending on her desires. Right now she wanted it to be longer so she could settle down and compose her thoughts about the terror she just left behind.
   She began to think about what had happened: The first time she was there it had been so beautiful and heaven-like. *What happened to that beautiful sky?* This time it was a dungeon and it was horrible! *Why was it a dungeon this time?* Since God was still out, there couldn't have been a judgement nor a hell, *so what had caused the difference?* So many questions.

Some friends waving at her as she passed brought her by back from her reverie. Then another couple smiled greetings; they were Jerry and Sandy this time although she had a slight recollection that at another time and place they had been different people with different names.
   People and things were often changing here, but she could always recognize them no matter how different they were. Every time she went out from her home many things were changed; sometimes in small ways, sometimes substantial so she saw her world with brand new eyes every day. Even her friends changed in many ways.
   It had taken her some time for her to realize that while things changed in appearance, their energy stayed the same, so she had to

learn to rely less upon the way things looked and more on how they felt; recognizing people and things as vibrations she learned to acknowledge them as one might to an old friend. (it was just the way it was here). It was really quite interesting once you got used to it, much like in a dream. Angela waved back to the energy that they represented rather than the image that they portrayed. She had many friends now, more than she could ever remember. It didn't take everyday conversations and being together to establish depth; some people and things just kept popping up in her relationships with a closeness or familiarity—*from some other life* she suspected. *I suppose I change too,* she thought, *but I never noticed.* Sometimes she wondered about this but most times she just accepted it just as the way things are here.

By the time she got home she was pretty well convinced that she neither needed nor wanted to return and face placement—*not if it means going back to that dungeon;* and with a contented sigh without breathing she walked inside. She was never quite sure if she was walking inside a home or inside of herself somehow; it was just a comfortable and familiar place for her to 'be'.

She visited with her friends, puttered around her home and garden and took nice walks and stuff like that; there was always fun and challenging things to do. Sometimes she mentioned her interest in going back to the Placement Office; the responses were always neutral, neither encouraging nor discouraging her to go; however none of them seemed to be interested in getting placed. *Why should I go to the Placement Office anyway, no one's pushing me.* It seems to be all right for people to just stay where they are; now she was pretty sure they were right to stay away.

After a time, *that time thing again*, she realized she was still troubled that she hadn't been placed. While she smiled cheerfully on the outside, inside she was not happy; trying to fit back into her life *or whatever it was*, was not really working. The image of her eyes reflecting back at her from the golden mirror pried itself into her thinking and dug into her mind drawing her back. *Could she go up, should she be down farther?* The question pounded at her brain; she was not happy not-knowing. The Placement Office *had to be* there for some reason and she couldn't ignore the inner pull to return. Angela had to find out; No, she wasn't comfortable with it at all.

God is out

The time she spent with her friends became different now; she still cared for them of course but in a different way; in the back of her mind she wondered if she really should be there with them at all. Try as she might, she simply could not rid herself of the urge to go back. The idea frightened her though; she certainly did not want to come across that dungeon again. *But the office had been so beautiful the first time, what could have cause the change?*

Wondering more and more about this, she thought maybe her moods were actually changing things. The more she thought about it, the more she was convinced that her state of mind and feelings had to be affecting the way things appeared, both here, now and at the Placement Office itself.

Remembering back, she recalled a day when everyone she met was in a good mood and everything worked out. That in itself would not have been cause for remembering except that the following day was just the opposite; people were unpleasant, annoying and whatever she tried to do was more difficult. Finally she had gone home to brood by herself. Mulling over the difference between the two days she had realized that for some reason she woke up in a bad mood that morning while the day before she had been happily singing as she went about her day. A saying came to her mind, "Give a smile, take a smile, Give a frown take a frown." *Could my state of mind play a part in all of this?* She could not escape the answer; t*his must be what's happening*.

Angela really didn't think she would go to hell at least she felt that it wouldn't be the result, but that was yet to be decided since God was still out. While the very idea of returning to the office brought fear shivers up her spine, the inner pull to return could not be denied. She began to think that she might actually try it again--without being scared of course.

Eventually she decided to go back to the Placement Office and try again. She plucked up her nerve and gathered her courage. Carefully she brushed her hair, put on just the right dress (and face). *Her shoes kind of hurt but they went well with the dress she had decided to wear.* Then making a final tuck and pat to her hair she took a deep breath-not breath, and opened the door. Stepping from the place she called home, she noticed jewel-like dew glinting from leaves like a million tiny lights; it was bright but not so bright as to make her squint. Everything shined with its own special brilliance. Angela loved being out in nature when she was alive, now she loved it even more. The bewitching plants and trees that dotted her landscape were different again today.

As she started to walk to the Placement Office, a pathway began to unfold in front of her. It was different somehow, It always was. *Things often change here;* sometimes in small ways and sometimes substantial so every day she got to see her world anew again.

Sometimes a gentle rain would fall on her as she walked upon the path, but she never really got wet. A breeze might blow but only gently rustling her hair. It was interesting that if she just wanted to stay nearby, a pathway would not appear.

Leaves lightly brushed her cheeks as she passed (the pathway was seldom very wide across). It was a nice feeling and usually she liked to walk slowly enjoying natures caress, but now she was focused on getting to the Placement Office, so gently she brushed the leaves aside and walked with determination following the opening pathway. Her footsteps did falter as the pathway opened onto the Placement Office and she was jolted into the reality of placement. Yes, she accepted that she had come again, to be placed.

She felt very brave to be at the Placement Office again, it took a lot of courage which was understandable; no one would be able to understand her special problems, desires or pain that she had felt. Yet still she had come (if reluctantly), to be placed.

She had to force herself to be humorous instead of frightened and it took a great deal of thought and mind control for her to do so. Upon entering the office she was laughing. Everywhere she looked there was merriment, *How can mere objects have so many funny expressions?* It *was* like the whole Office was laughing. Even the secretary was chuckling as if they were sharing a joke.

She stopped laughing soon after entering however; God was still out and she was back in the waiting room again. Picking up a magazine, she thumbed her way through, flipped it closed and began another, but she felt that something was pulling at her and she looked up to find her eyes staring back at her from the mirror.

Quickly she looked back at the book feeling as if she were being watched. She knew that this couldn't actually be happening, but she did not look up again.

After several hours, her mood was no longer cheerful and she was beginning to feel angry and left in a huff, - - again unfulfilled. But as she left, she noticed that the secretary and the Office itself, was still laughing. The trees lining the pathway seemed to be laughing as well, with limbs bending at their sides like washer women at the well.

The forest area directly around and closest to her was rigid and unsmiling however—while everything else was laughing, she was still angry; a stolid island surrounded by a laughing sea. Yes, it had to be her feelings making the changes because Angela wasn't laughing any more.

Days passed; sometimes days lasted so long that looking back on them she wondered if she had been weeks (or lives) instead; others ended just as soon as she wanted to sleep; *she didn't have to sleep of course, it was just a habit; like the non-breathing thing, sleep too was just a habit.*

No matter how she tried though, she couldn't get rid of the urge to return; *The Placement Office has to be there for some reason. What did I do wrong?* Laughing; she was laughing when she walked in, and everything laughed along with her, but she really wasn't in a funny mood at all, in fact, she couldn't actually remember how she had been feeling at the time but it certainly wasn't joy.

So Angela finally admitted that she wasn't being herself; *HE would have to have known, I need to get real*. She really had no doubt that her mood would affect what she would find on the other side of the door. Being in fear certainly had not worked, and forget about laughing. Probably the best thing to do was to simply be herself in a calm manner. While being calm would likely work, what would make her feel calm right now would be the idea of not returning to the office at all.

Before long Angela again found herself standing in front of the Placement Office. The same door that had protected her from the dungeon now stood closed in front of her. She did have her doubts; *what specter will present itself this time?* But Angela forced that thought from her mind. *All I have to do is to stay calm.* Calm - 1,2,3, in breath-not-breath, calm, 1,2,3 out breath-not-breath. Neither amused, nor fearful just calm. It was hard to do but she forced a slight smile on her face.

Pushing the great door open she peered around the carved edging into the office wondering what she would find. The office was beautiful this time, just beautiful, not extreme nor scary or funny, just beautiful; her feelings and mood were under control. There was a bit of a shock when she saw the sign on the desk though; God was still out.

The sweet old lady behind the secretaries desk led Angela to the waiting room and assured her that God would return soon. There was something about this old lady that struck her as familiar but she couldn't place the who, where or when of her. This time the secretary was a sweet old lady. Each time at the office there had been a different person behind the desk. Come to think of it, she had felt similar feelings about the other secretaries as well; she had just been too involved with her visit and caught up in the appearance of the office to notice them before. She had never really spoken with the secretaries but she couldn't help thinking that God changed secretaries as often as some people change their sox. Anyway, it didn't matter who was behind the secretaries desk, Angela was in the office to be placed, not to find new friends.

The door to the waiting room was similar to the one in front; all sculpted with intricate figures, But this one was different. The carvings on this door made the difference; each figure had a profound depth to it; like you could see into them somehow. There were faces there that she could almost remember, places and memories lodged just out of reach at the edge of her mind if she stared at them for a moment.

They seemed to be gesturing to her as she closed the door behind her.

Although the office kept changing the waiting room remained the same; plush yet comfortable. She figured that as usual it was going to be a long wait, so she cozied herself up on the large and comfy sofa. Determined to make it work this time, she took a magazine and settled down to wait. She even kicked off her too tight shoes. She would wait as long as it took and was not about to walk out again, and especially not in a huff.

For a moment she looked up from the magazine and caught her image staring back from the mirror. She really did like that mirror. *It isn't real gold,* she thought to herself not for the first time; *Is it?*

She chuckled as she remembered the other times when she had sat in front of the mirror; sitting prim, still and perfectly "smiled," as she waited for God to return and call her in. At first she had suspected that the golden mirror was a "two way," and that God was watching her from the other side. Then thoughts had raced through her head as she tried to remember the things she had done in front of the reflective surface. Now she laughed as she pictured the poses she had assumed in order to show God how cool and confident she was just in case HE really was watching. Finally she had inspected the mirror and found that it wasn't a 'two way' after all, then she felt foolish. But before long she began to feel annoyed; *If HE isn't behind the mirror, where the hell is He then? Is hell a swear word?* She wasn't sure, but actually at that point, she really didn't care: *Why didn't HE return? Just where does God go when he goes out anyway? Must have been called out on some emergency,* she thought; *perhaps a war or something like that. Whatever, it is it must be more important than placing me.* Finally she had gotten up and left with the dismal feeling of being ignored.

Now looking down at the magazine in her hands she realized that she had finished it. Flipping through the rest of them she saw that she had gone through them all—she didn't really read the magazines though, mostly she just looked at the pictures; she had always hated the idea of getting into a story only to have to leave it at the good part just to have a tooth pulled or something, and this; well this was like having the *big* 'tooth pulled, if you know what I mean.

Now there were no more magazines to look at; *the waiting room really did remain the same as she left it before.* The same magazines that where here before were still there where she had left them; one was left laying still opened; *Didn't I finish that?* she thought. The same thumbed-thru magazines and even the pillows on the couch were rumpled with her last imprint.

There were no more magazines to look at; nothing left now to ease the pain of waiting. Oh yes, it was painful for her; without

MF/BB 53

magazines to distract her, there was no longer anything to keep her from noticing the eyes staring back from the mirror; like magnets always there when she looked, drawing her in and holding her. She was frightened to look into those eyes too deeply; afraid of what she might see, so she would quickly look away but they were always there when she glanced back again.

Another bead of sweat worked its' way slowly down Angela's armpit; a telltale sign of the anxiety that lay beneath the calmness that she tried so hard to control. It was tempting to leave again but the secretary had specifically said that God would would return soon and Angela was determined not to be intimidated this time. *Waiting is the worst thing.* she though. *If only HE was already here it would be so much easier.* She just wanted to get this over with. More sweat was working to the surface.

She noticed now, that a strand of hair had fallen out of place. *Damn! - - Shit I said damn, damn I said shit! When will I ever learn not to swear?* Taking another deep non-breath she tucked her hair back into place.

When she first arrived she looked neat, sharp and even if she thought so herself, she looked great. It wasn't just her appearance that was in order, her mind was in order too; she knew the answers to whatever God might ask her, and (well most) of the reasons or excuses for all the bad things as well; she hadn't really been *that* bad.

Waiting always took its' toll though; first she would get nervous, then her planned answers would get confused, she would become tense, sweat and, and - - "That damned mirror! If only it wasn't right here in front of me!" This time she didn't even chastise herself for swearing.

Angela boosted herself up and straightened her skirt, her knees were a bit weak and she felt kind of shaky, but with a deep breath- not breath, she regained the reasonable facsimile of the calmness that she had when she entered the office. With another tuck to her hair and an adjustment to her girdle, she was ready to confront the secretary.

"Well, it looks like I've been stood up again, doesn't it" she said to the old lady. The words sounded wrong—too strong, but the tremble in her voice reminded her that she really was hurt, lonely and

God is out 54

frustrated too; she wasn't really strong and certainly not cool at all.

The old lady looked up; she had a warm smile, but tears seemed to be forming in her eyes. Angela remembered seeing that look before; somewhere sometime in the past, a bittersweet look; like a mother has as she pulls a sliver from a chubby finger stuck out to be made 'all better', a look that tries to tell a child who really doesn't understand, that sometimes things have to hurt a bit more before the pain will go away.

"Please stay Angel, just a little longer." The old ladies voice was thin with age but filled with care. The desire to melt into her arms was almost overwhelming, "but" Angela continued, "Who does God think he - -." The words choked within her throat. "Angel," that was what her mother used to call her. The old lady's eyes, and her words had found a place among Angela's memories forming a picture there.

There had been many tears shed when Angela left home so many years ago, *or was it lifetimes* It was hard to tell. Angela hadn't shed the tears of course, her mother had. "Please stay Angel," she had pleaded, "just a little longer." But Angela had been unyielding; the walls of the house where she had grown were closing in and it was time for her to go. "You're just thinking about yourself," she had shouted harshly. She looked past her mothers tears, and continued, "You have friends; you'll be fine. You'll get used to living alone, besides, I'll call you often." Then Angela kissed her crying mother on the cheek and left. The world was waiting for her, and she was ready for it. She knew she looked good; in fact, if she said so herself, she looked great. The world turned out to very good indeed, to Angela.

Oh, she did call her mother—probably not as much as she could or should have, but she did call. Then there was the call; not from her mother, but from Blanch, her mothers neighbor and friend who had been looking after her as she slowly died of leukemia. "She didn't want you to know," she said; "she didn't want you to worry."

The guilt had been almost unbearable. *Why hadn't her mother said anything about it? She would have stayed if she had known. How could she know when no one told her? She couldn't have known, so why did it hurt so bad?*

The reverie ended and Angela could see clearly now. "Mother," she cried falling on her knees in front of the old woman, "It's been you along, and I haven't been able to see it." Tears then mingled with tears, as mother and daughter found each other at last. Their tears washing away the hurt deeply buried within them both.

Her mother gently took her head and rested it in her lap. "Sometimes," she said as she gently stroked Angela's hair, "we can be very selfish and unkind when we keep secrets, even if it's meant to spare someone else pain. I knew I was to die, but I didn't realized just how soon I was to go. I thought I could tell you once you were settled down in your own life. I know now how much suffering I caused you by not telling you about my disease."

Angela felt her mother's hands lifting her face, and their eyes met. *My mom's here,* she thought, *and it's okay.* Her heart expanded inside *(and here it really did expand).* She touched her mother then just to be sure that she was indeed *here* with her, *now.*

Years passed or perhaps it was only seconds when she heard her mother saying, "You will find Him now Angel, I know you will." They embraced once more and Angela found herself in the waiting room; waiting again, - - for God.

Making herself comfortable on the couch (she was used to this now), she glanced back at her reflection in the mirror. *What was it about those eyes looking back?* They were irresistibly magnetic; mesmerizing and drawing her into them somehow. The pull was so great she became frightened and quickly looked away. Yet she was drawn back to the mirror again and again just the same. The eyes were compelling her, drawing her in. Gingerly she allowed herself to look back at the mirror. The pupils were like tunnels going deep within the mirror, *or was it into her soul?*

Rainbows began to appear, and paisley patterns formed within the mirror, floating and gently changing around everything. So far away, so near and so beautiful. She could not look away now. Then the images began to change; different forms began to take shape, sometimes just a bit; sometimes a lot. There was a depth to her *looking* now that was different; she was seeing *into* rather than *looking at;* a different way of perceiving indeed. Deeper she went and deeper she saw. Then the image changed.

Another face began to form as if from her memories: mixing its self with her own image, *Is this a reflection of me?* she wondered. *Am I looking into my past—another life perhaps?* But then she wasn't really living what might be called a life now. As she thought about it, she realized that from *here* there were several lives that she could look back upon as if it had been *the last life*.

But there was something very wrong in what she saw looking back from the mirror. "You don't love," she said aloud. As she said the words tears began to flow as she realized that she had spoken the words to and about herself. No she didn't love. It had become such a part of her personality that she really didn't think about it anymore. Expanding, the image began forming a reflection of her; distorted and pulled out of shape.

A man was on his knees in front of her; pleading and begging her to stay. "I love you," he was saying, "please don't leave." She could see herself in front of him as if it were happening at this moment; even to the disparaging curl of distain on her lips. She knew that he loved her and while she did like him his love was not returned. Now she was leaving. It was nothing to her, but everything to him. He loved her totally; Angela, *or who ever she was then*, lived only for the moment and for herself. Philip hadn't meant much to her; *yes, Philip had been his name*. She had never been demonstrative; always the receiver, so seldom the giver; a little out of balance; it could have been better if it had been some of both but that is how it happened.

No, she did not love and had never really loved, she didn't know how to love. She had repeated it over an over and whether or not it was true she had come to believe it. "I don't know how to love," she would say; she wore the words like a badge. What mattered now was that she was through with Philip and moving on; the fact that he was on the floor begging her meant little if anything to her. There had been others as she remembered now. She felt cold, not in her flesh but in her heart (the heart that she imagined). She was shocked seeing herself standing before the kneeling man; a statue without feelings. *How could I have been so cold and cruel?* Tears began to flow and her breath (if it could be called breath) was coming in short gasps. *What did I do to that poor man whose only problem was that he loved me?*

Then the mirror showed her several lives all blending together as if she were living each of them at the same time. She could see how her emotions and reactions had changed or stayed the same one life after another. Love was missing in all of them.

MF/BB 57

In another life, Angela had been born with a silver spoon in her mouth. It wasn't really silver as in well - - silver, it was silver in that she had always been beautiful. She could never get enough of being beautiful. As she grew older she learned how to make herself more enticing and spent hours in front of mirrors; it seemed as if she couldn't pass a mirror without looking at herself, adjusting her hair or something; she loved making herself look more beautiful, never caring more about her date than the impression that she might make on him. She seldom cared as much about anyone else as she did herself.

With the help of those rainbows she was seeing herself as she had been. *I kept saying that I didn't know how to love, but probably I didn't love because I wouldn't love; I was in love with myself and my own image.* Angela saw herself looking back from another place and time. She was kissing herself in a mirror. She had just finished getting ready to go out on a date. After admiring herself, she had impulsively kissed herself in the mirror before she left. It wasn't as if she were really involved with her date. It was mostly that she had wanted him to make a fuss over her. *That's really all that matters.* She might not even date him again, but then there were others waiting for her so it didn't matter.

A summarization of a life.

The *in-between* images faded away as Angela focused on herself in front of the mirror as she waited in the Waiting room. She thought of all the effort she had taken to prepare for this interview. She had even rehearsed. And here she was, still acting the same role as before; she had made the same preparations she use to use to get ready for a date, only this time the date was with God.

Angela had always thought of herself as being a good person; it hadn't occurred to her that just living a life without creating problems wasn't really being a 'good person' at all. in fact, her narcissistic way of life had been totally devoid of any real emotion. Now she saw herself stripped bare. The mirror looked back at her without compassion just as she had looked at those other's. She fell to her knees in front of the mirror, and grasped at her image. Then she leaned her head against the glass and cried until there were no tears left (nor any at all, truth be known). At least she had never had any children, maybe that was a blessing.

God is out

Slowly she looked back at the mirror. A lock of hair had fallen out of place; tears streaked her make up which ran down the front of her dress leaving wet spots in their trails. The more she looked, the more assured she was the lipstick shade was wrong for her dress after all. *What must God think of me?*

Jumping up on shaky legs, she made her way back to the couch and sat down trying to fix her hair and make up at the same time. *Go ahead,* the mirror taunted her, *pick at yourself, then you'll really mess it up.* Her mind was laughing at her now. "

A cigarette, that's what I need. She reached into her purse, but after fingering the familiar pack for a few seconds, she withdrew her hand and snapped the purse closed. *Why can't I smoke in here, there isn't any sign saying I can't. Why? What stops me?* In her mind, she went back to the day that she had died. (Or on the day she woke up here she could never be sure). She had died in a car accident. *What a time to die; the day before I was going to stop smoking. Inconvenient timing that's what it was.* Back from her musing she looked at the bowl on the table in front of her; It was beautiful and rounded like it could possibly be an ash tray, but; - - BUT! That word should be spelled with at least ten letters and given a meaning not unlike 'prison' or 'solitary confinement'.

Defiantly she pulled the cigarette pack out of her purse, but couldn't bring herself to light one. Then she laid the pack on the table next to the ash tray, which seemed okay to her for some reason. She wouldn't smoke but she *would* leave her pack there. How could she hide it? God would know anyway.

Looking back at her face in the mirror she saw there was a hint of a smile now. Then with a start, she saw the smile turn into one of panic as she realized *where she was and how she looked. How can I be here looking like this?* Her hair was a mess, her makeup was smeared, tear stains lined her cheeks and her dress, and sweat had managed to form half circles under the armpits of the now rumpled blouse. After all the preparing, *how,* she wondered *could I have ended up looking like this? I've got to get out of here,* she thought. Jumping up from the sofa she grabbed her purse and her cigarette pack, and headed for the door.

Then an echo within her mind came back to her; "You will find Him this time Angel, I know that you will." Angel; her mothers pet name meant so much more to her now.

Almost in defiance she looked again into the mirror,; *To Hell with it*, she thought. This time she remembered that she was in *His* waiting room and, "Yes, I said Hell." The look of shock that was reflected in the mirror changed to a look of defiance. "To hell with it," she barked again aloud.

Reaching for a cigarette she placed it in her mouth and lit it while watching her image in the mirror: *Why not?* she thought as she threw the match into the bowl, *Its me isn't it? This is who I am and what I do. I wanted to quit but I couldn't. He must know that I still smoke, he knows everything.*

There wasn't any taste of course, nor smell, nor any satisfaction at all from the cigarette truth be known; It was just an empty habit, but habit it was non the less without the means to enjoy it, *enjoy or fix;* those two words kept coming up to her now. She simply had the habit with no physical way to fulfill it. *Habits; what are habits anyway? A habit is something that you do each day, or each hour, or sometimes with each new breath. By doing the same thing repeatedly time after time a habit begins; by repeating it, it becomes a routine—a habit. Where had she heard that?*

It did start her thinking though; *I could start a new habit right now just by not smoking; it's empty and unfulfilling anyway.* Yes, she could start new right now if she wanted to, simply by putting the cigarette down and not smoking; but (that word again) with that thought she quickly sucked at her cigarette taking a long but un-fulfilling puff.

Her hair had become more untidy as was her make up; streaked with tears and mascara. Her mind was pretty shaken up as well. She pulled out a new tissue from her purse as she took another non-puff on her cigarette. Then she placed the butt in the beautiful bowl and began to wipe the tears from her face. Looking back at the mirror she saw herself as she had been in her own bathroom in front of her mirror.

I made myself up to impress God! She let out a breath-non-breath, and dropped her head in resignation. First it was with those who really did love her, now she had made herself up for God, and she had even rehearsed. Old habits do indeed, hang on.

Yet look at me. It was like seeing herself for the first time in front of the mirror. *Why should I try to straighten myself up anyway, for whom? For God? Surely not; I tried so hard but not for the right reasons, I'm messed up now. Fact is I look like hell!, I'm messed up because I cried real tears;* she trembled as she realized that she had cared enough to cry real tears even seemingly wetting the front of her dress; *and the sweat marks were from real emotions. I've finally been feeling real feelings and caring. It's me, without a mask; and I guess that's the only way it could be after all. I'm a mess because maybe I can learn to love after all.* The tears and the sweat were her imagination of course, but they served the purpose.

Then she reached into her dress, pulled out the foam breast enhancers and threw them into the crystal waste receptacle; at least it looked like crystal. *What if someone came in and saw them there?* She thought, and quickly retrieved them and shoved them into her purse. Now the front of her dress was sagging where the supports had been. She thought of quickly putting them back but pulling them from the purse and putting them back in without being caught was a long shot at best. Being caught replacing them would be even more embarrassing than having them found in the first place.

Angela was looking at her reflection. "Who needs placement anyway," she said out loud; "I like it here in this place; where ever this is. I'm happy here". She flushed as she realized that she didn't have to wait any longer. She smiled; a smile that seemed to glow all around her. And in the mirror she was surrounded with paisley rainbows. Her heart raced as she thought of the new adventures that waited for her now that she didn't have to leave this place. She got up from the couch and looked one more time into the mirror before she left.

She straightened her hair, took the tissue from atop the table where she had thrown it and began to straighten her face. *No need to look like a rag,* she thought. Then she noticed the cigarette in the bowl. She looked at it as it lay in that beautiful bowl. The cigarette was just there; it didn't really light and there wasn't any taste or smell. Sometimes it would get shorter though. Then with a big smile on her face, she reached over and squished the cigarette out in the bowl, then she tossed the pack inside the bowl to lay beside the empty tasting cigarette.

"Damned nice mirror," this time she had said it out loud." The outer office was empty and beautiful, but now it was "just an office." However, there was a kind of echo that floated around her as she walked toward the door. "Angle," that's what she had called me, and that is what I must be. "See you Mom", she whispered to the echo. Then she wiped a tear from her cheek, took a deep breath not breath and with a smile, walked from the office into the beautiful new world that waited outside.

Angela was gone now, the office was empty and the sign on the secretaries desk was changing itself from:

God is in
to
God is out - -
Please take a seat in the waiting room.

Part 2

You and your own relationship with that which is called, God

Who Am I?

God is out

During the late 1960s I took several "trips" on LSD, called acid. Slowly but surely, over the course of about a year I saw, faced and consequently confessed, 'sins' that I was reliving on the drug to friends who were with me.

I didn't realize it at the time but by confessing what I had thought of as sin, my mind was being cleared of past events that I had hidden away in the darker corners of my memories. Cobwebs of denial had been causing "blinders" to obstruct what I could see and understand.

While I had been experiencing things through my own distorted view of reality and truth, slowly my mind was being cleansed of the need for secrets and the blinders receded one by one, showing me who I really was instead of who I had imagined myself to be.

One manifestation that appeared to me on acid, was an intense vision of NOW. It was as if this moment in time and place stretched out in duplicated layers that changed just a bit as they expanded away from me. It looked in many ways like writhing worms imprinted with the forms of my environment. I was terribly afraid of the vision as it surrounded me. The vision was to pass but I always remembered it. Over the years I have come to determine that I had looked into another dimension into time itself.

I confessed what I was seeing to my friends who sat shivering before me. They were afraid of where I was in my mind, but confession it seems, is indeed good for the soul.

When I had no more to confess, I saw a vision that was so powerful I could barely stand it. It was a vision of my kitchen where I was standing at the time. But it shined with such a sacred *beingness* that I knew it was Holy. Looking out my window or around my kitchen or through the hallway to other rooms and my friends. We were all - - Holy. It was as if we were all standing on Mount Olympus of Greek mythology as ancient Gods.

To me, who had always thought of God as being a bearded old man on a throne; it was overpowering.

I could not accept this vision and I screamed; "Marshall, we are God!"

The moment finally passed, but I was changed forever.

"Know Thyself" was inscribed in the forecourt of the Temple of Apollo at Delphi. This aphorism has been attributed to almost a dozen ancient Greek sages and others throughout the ages.

Who am I ? A talk about an essence of god.

Delivered by Michael Fleming/Brahmacharya Baba at Thomas Institute of Metaphysics. Los Angeles, California November 6, 1983.

Have you ever stopped to think about who you are?
What kinds of things you are made of?
What it is that makes you, - - a "you"?

In essence, we are a product of all that we have been.
Everything that we have experienced has had some influence one way or other, upon who we are right now.

If we were to make a "recipe" of what we are made of it might go something like this:
We might start with a couple of cups of Environment;
- - surely the place where you grew up, the people that were around as you were growing, the ethnic and religious backgrounds and so forth, had a great to do with who you've become.
We might add a cup or two of the physical mental and spiritual gifts that we were born with. Now lets add a generous amount of parental influence. Surely before we left the cradle we learned that "no no" meant that we had done something wrong. And we knew how to get praise, with a smile perhaps; from a toothless mouth.
And then we might add varying amounts of friendships influence; the people we chose as our friends had a major impact on the direction of our lives; we grew from sharing experiences with each other.
We can spice our recipe with a teaspoon here and a tablespoon there of the person who said just the right thing at the right time which was exactly what we needed to hear at that moment.

And we have all been influenced by education in differing degrees; some with a lot and some with the lack of it. Certainly religious or spiritual participation or the lack of it have left its mark.

And then we might add a cup or more of that soul essence that we had as we came into this world and inhabited this particular body at this time and this place and in these conditions.

There are many things that we do habitually without even thinking about it that have their roots from the time that we were growing up. "Do this, don't do that; this is good that is bad," had a huge impact.
The food we eat and the way we eat it,
the type of clothes we wear, and the way we interact with others; all of these are habits.

Take these ingredients and blend them together for just as long as you have lived and you will have a recipe for *you;* and everything that you do every day is influenced directly by this recipe.

But if you stop to think about it; not all of this is really 'you' is it? *What happened to the person that you would have been if not for all the outside influence? Perhaps that person is just hiding behind habits imposed on you by others.*

As we grow, our individuality begins to assert itself and we tend to rebel in different ways; shrugging off some of those ways of living that have been foisted on us over the years; *much to the dismay of those who sought to guide us.*

In changing our ingredients we stir it up a bit and modify our way of living to be more in line with how we really feel about things. As you let go of those habits *that are not your own* you become more of what you were born to be; - - yourself.

It can be a difficult time when a person finds that the way they were raised isn't the way they want to live.

Leaving home creates a big change in ourselves and more directly it changes who and what we are; influenced now more by our own personal desires and decisions.

As you have the courage to reach into your "Being-ness" and change these habits, you learn more about who you *really* are by allowing more of your own true essence to shine though.

"To find your fortune is to find who you are."
(Naked Carmen 1968)

You are your fortune and your foundation. You are what you deal with in life everyday. And the more of *you* that is expressed the stronger you are. It's scary sometimes to become yourself, but that's all you can become really.

As days and years pass, we are matured by life, like a fine wine. Life takes all of these ingredients and blends them for just as long as you have lived and creates a YOU.

You are unique in every way. And every day is influenced by your "YOU-NESS" which is that within you that lets you know what you want, what you like and what you really feel. Finally, most of us learn that no one has been able to tell us how to live our lives, we've had to find that out by ourselves. No parent, friend, teacher or comrade, no matter how loving they might be - - No Bible, Koran, Torah or any other religious tract can tell you all of the truth. Truth is found within everything that is in your grasp; everything that you see and feel has its truth.

In the end it is you who must decide what fits and doesn't fit; it is you who must winnow the chafe from the grain with the input of life. If it seems right we generally accept it, If it doesn't fit, we generally let it go. It might be small things or it might be large but each of us have made these decisions to one extent or another based on the life and the person *that you* have created as you *have* lived it.

And so we come to judgment; we have made decisions in our lives: We have said "It does fit but I'll accept it" or "It doesn't' fit for me and I'll let it go." But just because you let it go, does not make it wrong; Just because it doesn't fit for you doesn't mean that for someone else, the idea might be a perfect fit. We have no right to judge someone else. We are all different with different points of

view and different ways of living.
We are all perfect. - - In reality you are perfect just as you are; With all your aches, pains and limitations - - and all your self doubts.

In all of the universe there has not been, there is not now and there will never be, a more perfect YOU than you are right now.

Being that which you are and expressing your "You-ness"
is the most Holy thing that you can do.
"You-ness" is you being YOU.

Just as an acorn is perfect, as it grows into an Oak tree. So are you perfect, as you try to succeed and you hit obstacles and you try again, and sometimes you succeed and sometimes you fail; you are still perfect as you grow into the oneness with your own "I am".

The more you find about your self and your essence
the more you will find about the essence of God.
Because man and God are really inseparable.

When Moses asked God's name at the burning bush the answer came back and it said,
"I AM".

And here we have a clue for those who would know.
"I AM" is not witnessed. "I AM" is experienced.
Moses didn't just hear "I AM",
Moses said it as well.
- - There is a mutual saying of "I AM".

When I was very young, I had a mental picture of God andI knew who God was. I had been raised a Mormon and had grown up with the Michelangelo idea that God was a man on a throne in heaven, and that someday I would be dragged before him, (kicking and screaming no doubt), to be judged and sentenced, for my sins. - -

But as I grew older I came to see a different God; A God without limitations.

The God that I had known before had a physical image and a form that I could envision.

But the God that I experienced filled my head so much that I could not contain the vision of it. It would not fit into my three dimensional mind..

What I had been taught in church was so much more limited than what I had experienced.

I knew that giving up the L.D.S. church was the most terrible thing I could do. I was going to go to a place called, *The Sons of Perdition*; a Hell, reserved for only those who leave The Church and I was afraid that I would end up in this hell.

And so I prayed, probably for the first real time in my life. With all my heart I prayed.

And a voice said: "
Oh don't worry, you don't have to give up The Church, just grow beyond it.

Then I was given a vision of many people worshiping in many ways; Jews in Temples, Muslims in Mosques, Christians in Churches, Buddhists in Temples. American Indians in Medicine Circles, Mormons in Temples and many more.

And each in their own way was perfect.

I was shown that It doesn't matter what you believe.

What matters is what you "do" with what you believe.

Hypocrisy is the error, not the belief.

I tried to define the God that I had experienced. Now this is not easy for no words can describe the Multidimensional God that I have seen.

One day it came upon me that if I could not find a description of the God that I had experienced, maybe I could define what God was not.

I picked up a rock and said, "This rock is not God".
And a voice came to me saying, "Who are YOU to say what is and is not GOD!" (Now this was very revealing.)

Then words that begin with "Omni" came to mind;
"Omniscient" – God was all knowing.

God is out

I could not conceive of a God that didn't' know everything. I couldn't say, "I've got a secret from God and he can't know", - it just didn't fit.

"Omnipotent". God was all powerful; surely the creator of the cosmos, who makes comets go through and not hit anything, who made planets, who made me and you along with the mosquitoes and the crabs, has to be all powerful.

"Omnipresent." that was a real big one for me, because god was everywhere. God was even in the air that surrounded me, Everywhere, - - Omnipresent.

I thought of this as being, - "God stuff". And the "God stuff" was all around me like a sort of cosmic jello that I flowed through like a swimmer swims through water, and it surrounded me the same way.

I realized that as it contains me it also contains my essence. My 'God stuff' contains me here, the lectern I am using, you, and the chairs you're sitting on. it contains my notes, it contains my home, although I don't see it. It contains my dog, my chores, the ones I've finished and the ones' I haven't. It contains it all.

If I were to disappear, if I were to just, 'not be,' there would be a hole left in exactly my shape reflecting me.
Not only would it reflect me, but it would contain my home and my entire being-ness.

"And man was made in the image of God."
    Does not God then, reflect the images of mankind?

And so, when someone says to me; "Go with God",
    I can stretch out my hands into this God-stuff and say, "I am".
    And so I say to you; "Go with God."

Michael Fleming/Brahmacharya Baba

Part 3

Combined works

Compiled and edited by
Michael Fleming/Brahmacharya Baba

This thinking is new, this is not a novel.

This part should be read slowly a sentence or phrase at a time. If you come to a point where you don't understand, just stop there, reading more will only serve to confuse you further. Come back to it later or move on to the next part. Hold off on reading more until you understand what you have already read.

I give as I can, receive and understand as you can. The price for knowledge is costly and I am trying to give it to you for free.

In order to understand these things you will have to pay a price. Each will be faced with that personal price and only you can decide what it is and whether you are willing to pay it or not. Learning and growing always comes with a price. Students pay by studying, adults pay by allowing their minds to let go of old, outdated and deeply held convictions that no longer work.

God is out

For those who have not read *Follow Your Heart*; very simply, at the age of 20 I became one of the first computer programmers in the world. I also became materialistic, selfish and self righteous. Then I met a hippie.

From the day I met John the hippie I began to live my life differently; with less materialism and more freedom, less involved with my own self and more caring for others.

Seeing the way the hippies lived and loved, compared to my life and the way I was living, jolted me into wanting to change and be more like them; they loved; themselves and all others as well, they shared everything that they had and who and what they were and how they lived. Plus they accepted everyone as they are without judging.

They taught me that *We are One*, also that *We are God*. They said, "If you have something, give it away, if it comes back to you, it is yours, keep it, If it doesn't, it wasn't yours to begin with".
I had been self centered, selfishly living my life, but the hippies also taught me to love.

The 'trips' that I had on LSD were like concentrated therapy sessions, they were very painful for me because I had to face the truth of my past.

"I cannot look away from things I wish I did not know."
Reign, Netflix

My life began to change as I faced the good the bad and the ugly of myself on acid trips and with the events of my life itself (also in *Follow Your Heart*). The more of myself that I faced and accepted the more I was able to see the whole "Me" as an entity separate and apart.

Then I had a vision that was so vastly overwhelming that it simply could not fit into my brain, therefore I called the vision, - - "God." I wandered around aimlessly for months; not knowing whether to live or die, and not seeing the value in either one.
MF/BB

Individuals who receive information in states of expanded

consciousness are those who already feel deeply within themselves connections not only with the earth itself, but with deeper realities. They do not accept answers given by others, but insist upon finding their own.

There is a fine impatience, a divine discontent that drives them on until the frontiers within their own personalities are finally opened. The knowledge gained must then be integrated by the physical personality, and yet by its nature, valid knowledge of this kind will shed out its light and make its own way. The energy generated by some such experiences is enough to change a life in a matter of moments, and to affect the understanding and behavior of others. Seth Speaks, 471

All personal contact with the multidimensional God, all legitimate moments of mystic consciousness, will always have a unifying effect. They will not isolate the individual involved, but instead will enlarge [their] perceptions until [they] experience the reality and uniqueness of as many other aspects of reality of which [they are] capable.

[They] will feel, therefore, less isolated and less set apart. [They] will not regard [themselves] as being above others because of the experience. On the contrary [they] will be swept along in a gestalt of comprehension in which [they] realize [their] own oneness with All That Is. SS 247

With that vision along with knowing the ways of the hippies, I knew that I had to change. I quit my job and gave my home and all of my belongings away and "stepped out" as the hippies use to call it, to live a completely different life.

Seeing myself as apart and separate followed by the vastness that I called God led me to conclude that, "I am me, and all that is not me - - is God"; a mirror of myself and my life; which also led me to believe that no two people can see the same God.

Your personal *One-ness* is something that no one else can re-create. You are a one of a kind event; there is no one less than, nor greater than, you yourself.

God is out

No man achieves good by worshiping another man nor God for in the worshiping he makes himself separate, and less.
As the Hippies used to say, "Peace brother, thou art god."

Soon afterwords my life began unfolding into a journey of ever changing lives, one after another almost like dying but without tasting death or laying down of the body.
This was the dawning of the Age of Aquarius, and those who embraced it were changed by the unfolding energies of love expressed by the Hippies, or love children as they were also known.

While living these ever-changing lives, I was constantly looking for a Guru or teacher who could teach me more about the vision that had led me on this strange journey. Surely, I thought, their must be someone who knew enough about what I had experienced that they could guide me. While I came upon several Gurus and very nice groups, I could find none who knew as much as I had come to know.

I was discouraged until one day I found myself wandering around my house, wishing for a spiritual experience, when I chanced upon a book that I had bought in the late 1960s. I put it aside during those years barely read, because I could not understand it at that time. Now I thought to try it again. So I began to read Seth Speaks as received by Jane Roberts. I had only read a few pages when I realized that what I was reading described exactly what I had experienced so many years before with the vision that I had called God. Seth was describing the Multidimensional Reality and at last I understood what I was reading.

While I enjoyed the book, there was a lot of unneeded dialog and I found the extraneous words got in the way of the clarity of the thoughts. So I began to highlight only the words that mattered to me; separating the 'wheat from the chaff' in order to more fully understand what I was reading.

When I finished the book I began to type the highlighted words. My intention was to be able to read only what I felt was important.

MF/BB

Once I began this process, the urge to continue grew inside of me; almost an obsession. Sometimes I would change a word or a phrase that I thought worked better, but as I lay in bed about to sleep that night, the word or sentence that I had changed would flash in my mind over and over until I went back to the computer and changed it back. In all cases the original words worked best.

I did the same with Neil Donald Walsh's Conversations with God series and other spiritual works with the same results.

Next I was guided to print the works and cut each phrase apart. Then to sort them by 'subject' and tape them back together, ignoring which book the thought had come from.
In this way I feel as if I was directed to do this work

"Combined Works" is a result of that undertaking.   MF/BB

Combined works is divided into five different parts;

1. Truth
2. Creating
3. Death
4. Judgement
5. god/God

Before you begin to read, please take a moment; sit calmly and breathe deeply, and push inside a little while picturing your mind expanding in order to understand what you are about to read. It wouldn't hurt to do this often while reading these works.

Please be gentle with yourself, not everyone is ready to understand this yet. It may well be that you put the book aside as I did with Seth Speaks so many years ago. Only to pick it up later and continue when you are ready.   MF/BB

The following phrases are identified by these notations:
SS x – Seth Speaks followed by page number
CG 1 x – Conversations with God volume 1, x = page number
GG x – Gnostic Gospels
MF/BB - Myself; physical and spiritual

Truth
What and where is truth?

"What I'm telling you is the truth!" Where have you heard that before? It may have been in your church, or it might have been your parents, perhaps your friends or a teacher. The words are probably not the same but the meaning is there. Most often these 'truths' are not the same either. So how are we to know what is actually true?   MF/BB

Leaders, Ministers, Rabbis, Priests, The Bible [the Torah, the Qur'an The Book of Mormon, and other Holy books]: Those are not authoritative sources. Listen to your feelings. Listen to your highest thoughts. Listen to your experience. Whenever any one of these differ from what you've been told by your teachers, or read in your books, forget the words; words are the least reliable purveyor of truth.   CG I 8

I realize that the previous phrase will be difficult for most people.
Here is where you must pay a price for knowing what continues. Think inside about what your belief system consists of; do you actually believe everything that has been taught? Is there any place where you do not actually agree? Here is were you make yourself stand out from the crowd. Accepting that you feel something different and owning it will help you begin to grow. Simple honesty with ones self is not easy but is so meaningful.

I once tried to send a greeting card to those that I love; my message was simple, "The greatest law is Love". I wanted to write it in as many languages as I was capable since I have many friends around the world. I sent emails to all of them asking for translations; While 16 answered with interpretations, many replied that it could not be interpreted into their language. "The greatest law is love"; this simple sentence; a keystone of the New Testament that Jesus of Nazareth was supposed to have taught, yet it is untranslatable in many languages. If this simple and necessary phrase cannot be translated, how can any written word, no matter how holy, be accurate?

MF/BB

Words are very limiting. (Let that sink in for a moment.)

No matter the good intentions of our leaders or teachers, words are still limited. So the questions are, if you can't trust words, what can you trust and how can we actually know which pathway to follow?   MF/BB

There are many teachers among you but the greatest reminder is the voice within you. The voice within is the loudest voice with which I speak, because it is the closest to you.   CG I 19,20

Many words have been uttered in My name. Many thoughts and many feelings have been sponsored by causes not of my direct creation. The challenge is one of discernment. The difficulty is knowing the difference between messages from God and data from other sources. Discrimination is a simple matter with the application of a basic rule:

> Mine is always your highest thought,
> your clearest word,
> your grandest feeling.
> Anything less is from another source.

The highest thought is always that thought which contains Joy.
The clearest words are those words which contain truth.
The grandest feeling is that feeling which you call love.
Joy, truth and Love. These three are interchangeable, and one always leads to the other.   CG I 4,5

My truth is in the whisper of the wind, the babble of the brook, the creak of the thunder, the tap of the rain. It is the feel of the earth, the fragrance of the lily, the warmth of the sun, the pull of the moon.

Listen to Me in the truth of your soul.
Listen to Me in the feelings of your heart.
Listen to Me in the quiet of your mind.
Hear Me, everywhere.   CG I 210

God is out 78

That may sound too simplistic for some. But when in doubt, calm yourself and go to a quiet place; one in nature is best. Then in this state, simply listen and observe.
Nature just being itself is a wonderful example of truth.   MF/BB

Whenever you have a question, simply know that I have answered it already. Then open your eyes to your world.
My response could be in an article already published.
In the sermon already written and about to be delivered.
In the movie now being made.
In the song composed yesterday.
In the words about to be said by a loved one.
In the heart of a new friend about to be met.
My truth and your surest help in time of need—is as awesome as the night sky, and as simple, incontrovertible, and trustful as a baby's gurgle. It is as loud as a pounding heartbeat and as quiet as a breath taken in unity with Me.   CG I 210

Truth is not found by going from teacher to teacher, church to church, or discipline to discipline, but by looking within the self. The intimate knowledge of consciousness, the "secrets of the universe" are not esoteric truths to be hidden from the people. Such information is as natural to man as air, and as available to those who honestly seek it by looking to the source within.
    SS XVIII

When it comes to religion, most of us are not taught to think for ourselves; instead, we are brought up to believe the same way that our parents and family believes.   MF/BB

You accept the experience of others as gospel, and then, when you encounter the actual experience for the first time, you overlay what you think you already know onto the encounter. In most cases, you don't want to make your parents, your schools, your religions, your traditions, or your holy scriptures wrong, so you deny your own experience in favor of what you have been told to think.   CG I 63

You place so little value on experience that when what you experience of God differs from what you've heard of God, you automatically discard the experience and own the words, when it should be just the other way around. CG I 4

Sometimes people hold a core belief that is very strong. When they are presented with evidence that works against that belief, the new evidence cannot be accepted, as it would create an extremely uncomfortable feeling, called cognitive dissonance. And because it is too important to protect the core belief, they will rationalize, ignore and even deny anything that doesn't fit in with the core belief. Fantz Fanon

If you want to know what's true for you about something look to how you're feeling about it. [Because] Hidden in your deepest feeling is your highest truth. CG I 3

There are countless differing religions, opinions, philosophies, teachers and teachings; many insisting that they are the one and only true pathway to Heaven or salvation or God, Allah, Yahweh, Elohim - - all of which are pretty much the same, no matter how different the trappings.

There is a lot of good in most philosophies but seldom does any theology completely match the feelings of those who say they follow the belief. Most blindly accept what they have been taught or told without questioning the validity or how it feels. Once a belief has been established the majority pick and choose the rules or laws they will follow and simply ignore the rest—usually a subconscious decision.

We all want to believe that what we have faith in is true. While some do not judge the way others feel, many think that if they are right, those who believe differently must be wrong.

The most important thing to do is to follow your heart. What feels good inside is the path that you should be following, if something feels wrong it is up to you what you do with it. The heart doesn't push; it simply lets you know what you feel.

If a teaching works for you, take it, use it, and make it part of your life. If it doesn't, just let it go without judgement, perhaps it will

God is out

be right for someone else.

If you follow your heart's direction you can honestly create your own your own personal way of living and more fully take charge of how you create your life. This will change for you over the years as you grow by the way, as do your beliefs and life patterns.

You living your life, is the pathway.
I grew up as a Mormon in Salt Lake City, so I know how it is to have a belief system where you are the only one right and everyone who does not believe the same — is wrong.

It is very challenging for a person to dispute the values that they have been raised with, but to blindly follow a way of life simply because it is how you were raised is limiting at best. MF/BB

I have not said, your values are wrong. But neither are they right. They are simply judgments, assessments, decisions. For the most part they are decisions made not by you but by someone else: Your parents, perhaps, your religion, your teachers, historians, politicians. Very few of the value judgments you have incorporated into your truth are judgments you yourself have made based on your own experience. Yet experience is what you came here for, and out of your experience you were supposed to create yourself. You have created yourself out of the experience of others. CG I 62

You cannot know God until you've stopped telling yourself that you already know him. You cannot hear God until you stop thinking that you've already heard God. CG I 8

Basically what this means is that we are often inundated by well meaning preachers of one kind or another beating their own beliefs into us from church pulpits or with every day conversations. When you come to this teaching you will do better if you open your minds to the possibility of a new belief system. Understanding grows with the ability to understand. MF/BB

Hold to your values and beliefs, and stay true to (them) so long as you experience that they serve you. They form the structure of your life. To lose them would be to unravel the fabric of your experience. Still, examine them one by one. Review them piece by piece. Hold them up to the light of public scrutiny. If you can tell the world who you are and what you believe without breaking stride or hesitating, you are happy with yourself.

Do not dismantle the house, but look at each brick and replace those which appear broken, (and) no longer support the structure.
CG I 61,62

So now it is time to take responsibility for yourself. It is no use to blame God, your parents or anyone else; the responsibility for your life is your own. We have all been born and raised differently. Each of us have differing gifts or challenges to overcome. How we face these conditions is also different for each of us.

If you don't like the 'pathway' you walk in life, it is best to change or confront it now while you have a body to do it with. Once you have left this body (having died), it is more difficult to do because you will no longer have the use of the body to use as a tool.

You cannot know truth until you face the truth within yourself.
MF/BB

Creating

If you were to design and/or produce something you could say that you created it. If you cook a nice meal or plan a party, you might also say that you created that as well. It is the same with a painting, a well composed photograph or writing a play, song or book. You could say you created a lot of things.

But what of your life? Do you not create your life as well? Maybe you think that you are a victim of the forces of the world that surrounds you; that you are limited by circumstances beyond your control. What if you were creating your own life and your own world without knowing it?
MF/BB

Most people are totally unaware of the part that they play in creating the world that surrounds them. CG I 75

If you believe that God is the creator and decider of all things in your life, you are mistaken. CG I 32

Everything you do has an effect not only upon your own life but it spreads out into more areas of living than you realize.

When you move, change jobs or graduate school among other things, it is easy to see that you are creating a new life for yourself and that your circumstances are affected by it;.

But the circumstances and people you leave behind are changed, as well as the people and circumstances of your new life.

But it does not stop there, our lives are affected in many different small ways without most people even thinking about it.

When walking down a street, most people pass by others without noticing; you don't exist for them and they don't exist for you. Many people don't make eye contact because they choose not to acknowledge other folks. But should you make eye contact with someone, you both know that it was done; you have acknowledged that each other exist just by making eye contact. Often this will lead to an encounter of some kind; it may be as simple as a mutual smile, or more. Either way subtle changes have taken place.

It has been said that the eyes are the windows of the soul, and so it is. So much is said with just a glance, or no glance.

When walking toward someone on the sidewalks, our eyes tell each other which side we will pass; hundreds of people can fill large areas without hitting one another because of this. What happens when someone is too busy looking at a smart phone or just looking at their feet? They bump into other people.

Think about a person who has a continual frown on their face. Imagine what their life must be like as people react to that frowning face. Now think about a person who has a wonderful smile. How do you think their day unfolds? In a totally different manner wouldn't you think?

What you say creates as well; have you ever said or heard someone say, "I'll worry about it later"? That plants a seed in the creative juices that could pop up—later as a strange feeling of unease. How about saying, "I'll deal with it later?" A better approach to say the least.

These simple things and more, can and often do create changes in our lives.

As we go about our days it is quite possible for something to go wrong; a person can cut you off while you drive, someone can push in front of you in line—many things. Later we can relive that event and become disturbed; if you catch this happening, you can change your mood very easily; by humming a tune or singing softly to yourself. Before you know it, you will feel better. People who hear you will also be affected in a nice way.

In order to understand these sections, it is necessary that you realize that there is more going on in this world than you currently realize.

God is out

The most important idea to be remembered is that no one thrusts the experience of any given lifetime upon you. It is formed faithfully according to your own emotions and beliefs.   SS 208

The deepest secret is that life is not a process of discovery, but a process of creation. You are not discovering yourself, but creating yourself anew. Seek, therefore, not to find out who you are; seek to determine who you want to be.   CG I 20

The responsibility for your life and your environment is your own. If you believe otherwise, then you are limited. As long as you believe your environment to be objective and independent of yourself, [or] that there is something or someone else out there 'doing it' to you, you disempower yourself to do anything about it [and] to a large extent you feel powerless to change it. Only when you say, "I did this," can you find the power to change it. The first step in changing anything is to know and accept that you have chosen it to be what it is.   SS 67, CG 136

You are the creator of your reality, and life can show up no other way for you, than that way in which you think it will. You think it into being. This is the first step in creation. Your thought is the parent which gives birth to all things.   CG I 52

Thought proceeds form.   MF/BB

Environments are not objective things—conglomerations of objects that exist independently of you. Personal environment and the physical world that you know, in a very real manner [are] the physical [manifestations] of your own thoughts, emotions and the senses that you use. They are quite literally extensions of yourself.
CG I 164, SS 27, 44,46

Whatever you put after the word "I" becomes the creative command. [You] produce what you call forth! You call forth precisely what you think, feel, and say. It's as simple as that.
CG II 12

In each life you are meant to check the exterior environment in order to learn your inner condition. The outer is a reflection of the inner. SS 211

When you align your thoughts

with a determined action [and] mental images accompanied by strong emotion, [these] are the blueprints upon which a corresponding physical object, condition or event, will in your terms appear.   This would apply whether the mental image was a fearful one or a joyful one.
If your turn of mind is highly intense and you think in vivid mental emotional images, these will be swiftly formed into physical events. Materialization [of these thoughts] will quickly appear, and therefore potentials for both constructive and destructive elements are high. The more intense your imagination and inner experience, therefore, the more important it is that you realize the methods by which this inner experience becomes physically real.
SS 78,80

If you are of a highly pessimistic nature, given to thoughts and feelings of potential disaster, then these thoughts will be quite faithfully reproduced in [your] experience. CG I 79

If you think thoughts of illness or disease (or continuing anger, hatred, and negativity, your body will translate these thoughts into physical form. CG I 182

If, on the other hand, your feelings and subjective experience are fairly well balanced, fairly optimistic and creative in a constructive manner, then it will seem to you that you have been blessed with unusual luck, for your pleasant suppositions come to pass so quickly. CG I 79

All you see in your world is the outcome of your idea[s] about it.
Your own life is the way it is because of you and the choices you have made or failed to make. CG 1 75,50

If you think this a far fetched idea, think about what happens when you dream. Your dreams always have some kind of setting

or landscape in them that surrounds you as the dreamer. Where did this environment come from if you didn't create it?   MF/BB
Your thought about something is creative, and your word is productive; your thought and your word together are magnificently effective In giving birth to your reality.   CG I 10

Because you create what you are, your life will of necessity be a reflection of who you are.   MF/BB

You are always in the process of creating every moment, every day. You are a big creation machine, and you are turning out a new manifestation literally as fast as you can think.   CG I 35

This could be an overwhelming thought if you over-think it. If everything is a statement of who you are, what about when you are taking a nap? "OK universe, my body is tired right now and I need to sleep a bit." Or eating? Same thing, "My body needs food to live." Or maybe it's about a habit like smoking, drinking, drugs or sexual addiction? "I'm doing this because I like it," or, "I am hooked on this." All of this is simply an honest statement to the universe of who you are at this moment, nothing more, nor less.

Think about it; what are you creating today?

Try to be aware of the thoughts, feelings and actions that you are experiencing; not in judgement, but to be able to ask yourself if this is the grandest experience of who you are, here and now?
MF/BB

There is only one reason to do anything; as a statement to the universe of who you are. Used in this way, life becomes self creative, and you use life to create your self as who [and what] you are and who you've always wanted to be.   CG I 37

There is a price for procrastination; it is having to do now, what could have done earlier. You are in this body at this time to learn to do things the hard way, (three dimensional limitations). When you no longer have a body, it is easy to create something by thinking it into being; the lessons learned are only as valuable as the amount of energy you had to use to make it happen. MF/BB

You are learning to be co[-]creators. You are learning to be gods as you now understand the term, [and how] to handle the energy that is yourself for creative purposes. {Also} you are learning responsibility, the responsibility of any individualized consciousness. SS 63

We seem to live in a three dimensional world and many people believe that this limited world is all that exists. But science has shown time and again that this is not the case. MF/BB

Your physical senses force you to translate experiences into physical reality—a three-dimensional [perception] of reality. Using physical senses, you can perceive reality in no other way.
SS 27,93

The keyword here is *perceive*. While it may occasionally seem that we are moving through life without causing a ripple, quite the opposite is the case. There are many different and equally valid dimensional manifestations that are affected. It is possible under certain conditions, to break through the three dimensional barrier and experience other dimensions; however this experience stuffs the three dimensionally oriented mind, often overwhelming it. People who have experienced this vision often refer to it as God.
MF/BB

The personality has within it the ability not only to gain a new type of existence in the physical reality but to add creatively to the very quality of its own consciousness. SS 79

Do you want your life to truly "take off"? Then change your idea about it. Think, speak, and act as the god you are. CG I 74.75

When you are here, honestly with yourself in this place and at this time, you act with the strength of ten, because you are centered in the here and the now, with the full power of yourself, which is all that there is, really. MF/BB

God is out

Seek to create change not because a thing is wrong, but because it no longer makes an accurate statement of who you are.   CG I 36
Here is an exercise:
Go first to your Highest Thought about yourself.
Imagine the you that you would be if you lived that thought every day. Imagine what you would think, do, and say, and how you would respond to what others do and say.

Now, having seen the differences between where you are and where you want to be, begin to change, consciously change your thoughts, words, and actions to match your grandest vision. This will require tremendous mental and physical effort. It will entail constant, moment to moment monitoring of your every thought, word, and deed.

Begin at once to imagine it the way you want it to be—and move into that. Check every thought, word, and action that does not fall into harmony with that; move away from those. When you have a thought that is not in alignment with your higher vision, change to a new thought, then and there. When you say a thing that is out of alignment with your grandest idea, make a note not to say something like that again. When you do a thing that is misaligned with your best intention, decide to make that the last time. And make it right with whomever was involved if you can.
                                                                          CG I 77,78

Life will "take off" for you when you choose for it to. You have not so chosen as yet. You have procrastinated, prolonged, protested. Now it is time that you promulgated and produced what you have been promised. To do this, you must believe the promise and live it. You must live the promise of God. The promise of God is that you are His son, Her offspring, Its likeness. His equal.   CG I 75

If you want something badly enough, just picture it as already being a real situation, then feel, act and expect it and proceed as if it were so. Doing this you can sometimes cause what is called, a miracle.   MF/BB

The usual method of creation for most human beings is a three-step process involving thought, word, and deed, or action. First comes thought, the formative idea: the initial concept. Then comes the word. Most thoughts ultimately form themselves into words which are often then written or spoken. Finally, in some cases words are put into action, and you have a result; a physical world manifestation of that which started with a thought.

CG I 164

This actual matter is the creation of pure thought—the work of your mind, the higher mind aspect of your three-part being. [Mind, body and spirit or soul] This matter is a coagulation of a million billion trillion different energy units into one enormous mass, controllable by the mind. You really are a master mind.

CG I 182

Life is an ongoing process of creation. You are creating your reality every minute. The decision you make today is often not the choice you make tomorrow. Yet here is a secret of all Masters: keep choosing the same thing over and over until your will is made manifest in your reality.

CG II 10

When you "make up your mind" about something, you set the universe into motion. Forces beyond your ability to comprehend, far more subtle and complex than you could imagine are engaged in [the] process. Change your mind all you want. Yet remember that with each change of mind comes a change in the direction of the whole universe.

CG II 10

Once you fully start something with vision and commitment, then follow through with action, the entire universe will respond with help. Think about it; what do you want to create in this life?

When you change your mind or get into different projects, you send out conflicting messages, resulting in less than optimum results.

MF/BB

You seek a newer world. Seek it no longer. Now, call it forth.

CG I 76

From the new thought springs [new] experience, and the body

begins living a new reality as a permanent state of being. Your body, your mind, and your soul [spirit] are one. In this, you are a microcosm of me. You see now how I am the beginning and the end of everything, the Alpha and the Omega. CG I 97

Individual consciousness is powerful enough. You can imagine what kind of creative energy is unleashed whenever two or more are gathered in my name. And mass consciousness? Why, that is so powerful it can create events and circumstances of worldwide import and planetary consequences. CG I 35

When you are together with people of like minds, you can come to understand that you are co-creating the world around you with them. Take that one step farther and you can see that our whole world is a co-created event. MF/BB

[What we call] worldwide calamities are the result of worldwide consciousness. CG I 32

I do not will these things into being, I merely observe you doing so. And I do nothing to stop them because to do so would be to thwart your will. CG I 32

You are not choosing them anymore than I am choosing them. Like me, you are observing them, and deciding who you are with regard to them. SS 80

[As such], There are no victors in the world and no villains. And neither are you a victim of the choices of others. CG I 35

And now we come to prayer. Many people pray regularly, many, only in an emergency, "I know I have not prayed much but - - ". There are many kinds of prayer. When you want something, there is something that is important for you to know. MF/BB

You will not have that for which you ask, nor can you have anything that you want. This is because your very request is a statement of lack, and you're saying you want a thing only works to produce the experience, wanting in your reality.

The process of prayer becomes much easier when one understands intuitively that the request itself is not necessary. Then the prayer is a prayer of gratitude. CG I 11

The correct prayer is therefore never a prayer of supplication, but a prayer of gratitude. When you thank God in advance for that which you choose to experience in your reality, you, in effect, acknowledge that it is there. Thankfulness is thus the most powerful statement to God. A prayer is nothing more than a fervent statement of [that which] is so. Every prayer, every thought, every statement, every feeling— is creative. To the degree that it is fervently held as truth, to that degree will it be made manifest in your experience. CG I 11,12

No one can say you are beautiful until you say you are beautiful, no one can say you are strong until you say you are strong, no one can say you are wise - - . Oh, they can say it
but it is only real when you are the one who says it.

In the beginning there was thought. MF/BB

God is out

Ah, and now we come to death.

How will you come to death? Will you be afraid?
Have you been killed?
Have you held on beyond the time it might have been easier?
Do you think there will be nothing else to face?
Do you welcome this release from life
   or do you fear the loss of life as you know it?
Maybe you believe there will only be dark emptiness?

Will you know of it or will you just be unaware?

Contrary to popular or religious belief,
each of us will face a different and personal experience
after leaving the body,
   - - or maybe experience nothing at all.

Welcome to death.
Time was when death was the thing to fear.

And now
it is the thing to be.

There are many
deaths and births
in living.

The gasping of the breakthrough
following the fright at the end.
     "Yet do I long for thee; - - - to be cleansed".
        And as I long, I know that death is not a cleansing,
          - - it is a moment,
    - - and things go on, changed/not changed,
        and the moment is behind me, - - - again."

                              Michael Fleming/Brahmacharya Baba

MF/BB

We call them spirits; those who have passed away, but they are only in a different realm, a different dimension which is right in front of us.

I have heard spirit several times: When I heard, "Oh, don't worry, you don't have to leave the church, just grow beyond it." After I had the vision of God and knew I'd need to leave the Mormon Church. When my friend, Mike, said "Michael!" As I was trying to contact him at his funeral. It was his funeral after all. "He has AIDS," as I was about to get into bed with someone who died within the year. And "Well I'll be," From Bob, (a friend who had recently died) as I entered The Redwoods with Rodger to deposit remains of those who wanted to be remembered.

I have seen spirit when I was having a beer with my friends, Margie and Bob when a form appeared to me. "There is someone else here," I said; "She's wearing a cowl but she is not a nun." Margie said. "She is my sister, she died of cancer and wore a head covering to hide her bald head before her death."

I have felt spirit when my friend and ex-house keeper blew a draft of wind at me as her casket passed in front of me. I had been thinking 'poor her' thoughts, but as she passed in front of me I remembered that she used to go and pray for and with the poor and afflicted, and in her own apartment she let her son and his wife have her bedroom as she slept on the couch."NO," my thoughts came to me; she is just fine for she has done so much good." At that time; when her casket was passing before me and I was thinking these thoughts - she sent a puff of air to brush my cheek.

I have worked with the Spirit made flesh, with the hippie group who sent me upon this journey.

Spirits are very close to me, and they are to you as well.
All you have to do is accept and know.

Death - a process of living.

Life is a state of becoming, and death is a part of this process. MF/BB

Birth is much more of a shock than death. Sometimes when you die you do not realize it, but birth almost always implies a sharp and sudden recognition. So there is no need to fear death. SS 18

Though you do not realize it, you are often "dead," even amid the sparkling life of your own consciousness. SS 139

You are alive now, a consciousness knowing itself amid a debris of dead and dying cells; alive while the atoms and molecules of your body die and are reborn. From [these] tissues new life will spring.
CG I 182, SS 140

Every cell of your body changes every several years. You are quite literally, not the same person you were a few years ago. The body that you have now does not contain one particle of physical matter that it had, say ten years ago. The body that you had ten years ago, my dear readers, is dead. CG I 182, SS 140

You are alive despite, and yet because of, the multitudinous deaths and rebirths that occur within your body in physical terms. If the cells did not die and were not replenished, the physical image would not continue to exist. SS 138

Death of physical tissue is merely a part of the process of life as you know it; a part of the process of becoming. SS 140

The mind creates out of it's continuing thought about who you are. CG I 182

Your consciousness [also] flickers about your ever changing corporeal image. While it seems to you that your consciousness is continuous, this is not so. It also flickers off and on. Its focus is not nearly as constant as you suppose. SS 138

I am using your own terms here. By "dead," I mean completely unfocused in physical reality. There are pulsations of consciousness, though again you may not be aware of them. For one instant your consciousness is "alive," focused in physical reality, [and] the next instant it is focused somewhere else entirely, in a different system of reality. It is unalive, or "dead" to your way of thinking. The next instant it is "alive" again, focused in your reality, but you are not aware of the intervening instant of unaliveness. Your sense of continuity therefore is built up entirely on every other pulsation of consciousness. In the same way, atoms and molecules exist so that they are "dead," or inactive within your system, then alive or active.

What you call death is simply the insertion of a longer duration of that pulsation. SS 139

What happens at the point of death? Basically there is not any particular point of death even in the case of a sudden accident.

What the question means to most people [and] what you [really] want to know is, "What will happen when I am not alive in physical terms any longer?" What happens when [my] consciousness is directed away from physical reality, and seems to have no image to wear?

What will I feel? Will I still be myself? Will the emotions that propelled me in life continue to do so? Is there a heaven or a hell? Will I be greeted by gods or demons, enemies, or beloved ones? Most of all the questions mean: When I am dead, will I still be who I am now, and will I remember those who are dear to me now? SS 138, 140

There is no one answer, for each of you is an individual. The kinds of deaths have much to do with the experience that consciousness undergoes. Also involved is the development of the consciousness itself. SS I 40, 41

Actual death is no problem. The dying however, is what tends to concern people. MF/BB

The ideas that you have involving the nature of reality will strongly color your experiences, for you will interpret them in the light of your beliefs, even as now you interpret daily life according to your ideas of what is possible and what is not possible.   SS 141

Close to [physical] death, the consciousness realizes that it can no longer express itself through the medium of the body.   SS 133

Your consciousness may withdraw from your body slowly or quickly, according to many variables.   SS 141

Some individuals remove their focus from physical life, leaving the body consciousness alone, others stay with the body until the last moment.   SS 230

Those who have not identified their consciousness with the body completely find it much easier to leave it. Those who have hated the body find, strangely enough, that immediately after death they are quite drawn to it.   SS 154

You may after death utterly refuse to believe that you ARE dead and continue to focus your emotional energy toward those you have known in life. If you have been obsessed with a particular project, you may try to complete it.   SS 154

It is possible for an individual who has died to completely misinterpret the experience and attempt to reenter the corpse. This can happen when the personality identified himself almost exclusively with the physical image.   SS 154

Those who "over identify" their consciousness with their body can suffer self-created torment for no reason; lingering about the body, indeed, quite the forlorn soul, thinking it has no other place to go. [Or] he can easily panic, thinking that all expression is therefore cut off. Such a belief is a severe psychological experience. What happens instead is that you find consciousness quite intact, and its expression far less limited than it was before.   SS 129, 133

The fear of death can cause you (to) lower your consciousness so that you are in a state of coma, and you may take some time to recover. SS 141

You may or may not realize immediately that you are dead in physical terms. SS 141

When life after death is completely denied, the problem is somewhat magnified. An individual can be so certain that death is the end of it all, that oblivion, though temporary, results.
SS 141,147

A personality who simply cannot accept what they experience after death, could just attempt to go right back to the three dimensional existence. Not a good thing at best. MF/BB

Suffice it to say that emotional focus toward physical reality can hold you back from further development. SS 154

All of these circumstances [and more] then may or may not occur according to the individual involved. However, after leaving the physical body, you will immediately find yourself in another. This is the same kind of form in which you travel in out of body projections, and again let me remind my readers that each of them leaves the body for some time each night during sleep. This form will seem physical. It will not be seen by those still in the physical body; however, generally speaking, it can do anything that you do now in your dreams. Therefore it flies, goes through solid objects and is moved directly by your will. SS 155

[The] image will appear physical to you as long as you do not try to manipulate within the physical system with it. Then the differences between it and the physical body will become obvious. SS 142

Most individuals after death choose a more mature image that corresponds to the peak physical abilities. SS 155

God is out

Certain images have been used to symbolize transition from one existence to another, and many of these are extremely valuable in that they provide a framework with understandable references.

The crossing of the River Styx is such a one. The dying expected certain procedures to occur in a more or less orderly fashion. At death, the consciousness hallucinated the river vividly. SS 141

Mass religious movements have for centuries fulfilled [this] purpose, in giving man some plan to be followed.

In periods where no such mass ideas are held, there is more disorientation. SS 147

Human religions are so popular. It almost doesn't matter what the belief system is, as long as its firm, consistent, clear in its expectation of the follower, and rigid. Given those characteristics, you can find people who believe in almost anything. The strangest behavior and belief can be [and] has been attributed to God. It's God's way, they say, God's word. And there are those who will accept that gladly. Because, you see, it eliminates the need to think. CG I 152, 3

Christianity has believed in a heaven and a hell, a purgatory, and a reckoning; and so at death, to those who so believe in these symbols, another ceremony is enacted, and the guides take on the guises of those beloved figures of Christian saints and heroes.
SS 146,7

The familiar parables, for some, will be gradually weaned away from them. SS 153

A belief in hell fires can cause you to hallucinate Hades conditions. A belief in a stereotyped heaven can result in a hallucination of heavenly conditions. You always form your own reality according to your ideas and expectations. Such hallucinations [however] are temporary. SS 141

There are those who hypothesize that upon death the body and the mind are dropped. The body and the mind are not dropped. The body changes form, leaving its most dense part behind. You [will] find consciousness quite intact, and its expression far less limited than it was before. CG I 181, SS 133

There is an initial stage for those who are still focused strongly in physical reality who need a period of recuperation and rest. On this level there will be hospitals and rest homes. The patients do not yet realize there is nothing wrong with them at all.

In some cases, the idea of illness is so strong that they have built their earthly years about this psychological center. They project ill conditions upon the new body as they did upon the old one. Delicate probing of the psychological processes is necessary, and the variety of hallucinations in which you may become involved is endless. SS 149

Many individuals do not need to pass through this particular period. You may call this mass hallucination if you will. The fact is that to those encountering that reality, the events are quite real.
CG I 152,153

Vivid hallucinations may form experience quite as real as any in mortal life; I have told you that thoughts and emotions form physical reality, and they form after-death experience. SS 146

It is possible for example to lose yourself momentarily in the hallucinations that are being formed. SS 149

You are not left alone in mazes of hallucination. Such hallucinations, I assure you, are temporary. SS 141

There are always guides to help you understand your situation, but you may be so engrossed that you pay them no heed. SS 154

Guides will helpfully become a part of your hallucinations, in order to help you out of them, but hey must first of all get your trust. Then with this as framework, and in terms that they can understand, such individuals are told the true situation. SS 147

All of these hallucinatory activities take place usually some short time immediately following death. Some individuals are fully aware of their circumstances, because of previous training and development, they are ready after a rest.

If they desire, to progress to other stages. They may, for example, become aware of their own reincarnational selves. They may deliberately now hallucinate, or they may "relive" certain portions of past lives if they choose. CG 1 150

In one way, your physical existence is the result of mass hallucination. Vast gulfs exist between one man's reality and another's. CG 1 150

Your experience is not *The right way*, nor is it *the wrong way*, it is just what it IS for you. Others will be experiencing their own realities. MF/BB

The spirit is never in a state of nothingness. It is very important to understand that consciousness is never extinguished. SS 130, 1

You are not bound to any category or corner of existence. Your reality cannot be measured any more than mine. SS 422

Consciousness, yours and mine, is quite independent of both time and space. And after death you are simply aware of the greater powers of consciousness that exist within you all the time. SS 129

[Some] have to learn about certain laws of behavior; the creative potency of their thoughts or emotions. An individual may find himself in ten different environments within the flicker of an eyelash, never realizing that his own thoughts are propelling [them] quite literally. CG I 147

There is no time lag, as their must be in the three-dimensional system, between the initiation of such thoughts and their materialization. CG I 153

You may or may not be greeted by friends or relatives immediately following death. This is a personal matter as always. SS 144

Your true feeling toward relatives who are also dead will be known to you and to them. There is no hypocrisy. You do not pretend to love a parent who did little to earn your respect and love.

Telepathy operates without distortion so you must deal with the true relationships that exist between yourself and all relatives and friends who await you.

You may find that someone you considered an enemy actually deserved your love and respect for example, and you will treat him accordingly.

You will not be automatically wise if you were not so before, but neither will there be

a way to hide from your own feelings, emotions, or motives. Whether or not you accept inferior motives in yourself or learn from them is still up to you.

For those of you who are lazy I can offer no hope: death will not bring you an eternal resting place. You may rest, if this is your wish, for a while. Not only must you use your abilities after death, but you must face up to yourself for those you did not use during your previous existence. SS 143

Consciousness must use its abilities. The boredom and stagnation of a stereotyped heaven will not for long content the striving consciousness. SS 141

Your personality as you know it will indeed persevere, and with its memories, but it is only a part of your entire identity, even as your childhood in this life is an extremely important part of your present personality, though now you are far more than a child.
SS 44

Then there is a period of self-examination, a rendering of accounts, so to speak, in which [you] are able to view [your] entire performance, [your] abilities and weak points and to decide whether or not [you] will return to physical existence. CG I 150

You examine the fabric of the existence you have left, and you learn to understand how your experiences were the result of your own thoughts and emotions and how these affected others. Until this examination is through, you are not yet aware of the larger portions of your own identity. SS 144

At some point you have to stand up and express that which you are. This is simply a process of taking a toll of just what and where you are in evolution at this point. Nothing more nor less, then deciding where you want to go from here. MF/BB

When you realize the significance and meaning of the life you have just left, then you are ready for conscious knowledge of your other existences. What you are begins to include what you have been in other lives, and you begin to make plans for your next physical existence if you decide upon one [or] you can instead enter another level of reality. SS 144

This is not, incidentally, necessarily any kind of somber endeavor, The after-death environments are not somber at all. To the contrary, they are generally far more intense and joyful than the reality you now know. You will simply be learning to operate in a new environment in which different laws apply, and the laws are far less limiting than the physical ones with you now operate.

Even these experiences will vary and this state [too] is a state of becoming for many will continue into other physical lives. [While] some will develop their abilities in different systems of reality altogether, and so for a time [may] remain in their "intermediary" state. SS 142

You don't have to do anything. If you enjoy life at this level, if you feel this is the ultimate for you, you can have this experience over and over again. In fact, you have had it over and over again for exactly that reason. CG I 149

Should you choose to return to this experiencing opportunity that you call life on Earth, your divine self will once again separate its true dimensions into what you call body, mind and spirit.
As you undertake to inhabit a new physical body here on Earth, your ethereal body (as some of you have termed it) lowers its vibrations [and] slows itself from a vibration so rapid that it cannot even be seen, to a speed that produces mass and matter. CG I 181

So you see, the possibilities are indeed endless. That which may have been seen as an ending is instead a door opening into unlimited potentials. MF/BB

God is out

What follows is a story told by Seth. MF/BB

At one time – in your terms, I myself acted as a guide; as in a sleep state Ruburt[1] now follows the same road. The situation is rather tricky from the guide's viewpoint, for psychologically utmost discretion must be used. One man's Moses, as I discovered, may not be another man's Moses.

I have served as a rather creditable Moses on several occasions, and once, though this is hard to believe, to an Arab. The Arab was a very interesting character, by the way, and to illustrate some of the difficulties involved, I will tell you about him.

He hated the Jews, but somehow he was obsessed with the idea that Moses was more powerful than Allah, and for years this was the secret sin upon his conscience. He spent some time in Constantinople at the time of the Crusades. He was captured, and ended up with a group of Turks, all to be executed by the Christians, in this case very horribly so. They forced his mouth open and stuffed it with burning coals, as a starter.

He cried to Allah, and in greater desperation to Moses, and as his consciousness left his body, Moses was there.

He believed in Moses more than he did Allah, and I did not know until the last moment which form I was to assume.

He was a very likable chap, and under the circumstances I did not mind when he seemed to expect a battle for his soul. Moses and Allah were to fight for him. He could not rid himself of the idea of force, though he had died by force, and nothing could persuade him to accept any kind of peace or contentment, or any rest, until some kind of battle was wrought.

A friend and I, with some others, staged the ceremony, and from opposite clouds in the sky Allah and I shouted out our claims upon his soul, while he, poor man, cowered on the ground between us. Now while I tell this story humorously, you must understand that the man's belief brought it about, and so to set him free, we worked it through.

---

1 Rupert is Seths name for Jane Roberts who received this text.

I called upon Jehovah, but to no avail, because our Arab did not know of Jehovah, only of Moses, it was in Moses he put his faith. Allah drew a cosmic sword and I set it afire so that he dropped it.
It fell to the ground and set the land aflame. Our Arab cried out again. He saw leagues of followers behind Allah, and so leagues of followers appeared behind me. Our friend was convinced that one of the three of us must be destroyed, and he feared mightily that he would be the victim.

Finally the opposing clouds in which we appeared came closer.
In my hand I held a tablet that said: "Thou shalt not kill." Allah held a sword. As we came closer we exchanged these items, and our followers merged. We came together, forming the image of a sun (spelled out), and we said: "We are one."

The two diametrically opposed ideas had to merge or the man would have no peace, and only when these opposites were united could we begin to explain his situation. SS 149

Judgement, --
the final test - or is it?

It may well be that for most people, judgement is the greatest fear, even surpassing the fear of death itself in most cases.

Will you be dragged, knees shaking, before a great throne where a huge bearded man looks down upon you with distain?

Will you just end up in a fiery place where there is screaming echoing all about you?

Maybe you will find a smiling Saint Peter who will lead you through great and beautiful pearly gates into a place where happy people with white robes dance on tip toe from one puffy cloud to another.

Maybe only the blackness of oblivion will follow this life just left.

Where will you find yourself?
Or will you not find yourself at all?

MF/BB

If you believe that God is some omnipotent being who hears all prayers; says, "Yes" to some, "no" to others,
and "maybe, but not now" to the rest, you are mistaken.
By what rule of thumb would God decide?　　　　　　CG I 13

"God is a loving God", you say, but if you break His commandments, he will punish you with eternal banishment and everlasting damnation.
　　You have forgotten what it was like to be loved without condition. You have projected the role of 'parent' onto God, and have thus come up with a God who judges and rewards or punishes. But this is a simplistic view of God, based on your mythology. It has nothing to do with who I am.　　　CG I 17

God created the process of life and life itself as you know it. Yet God gave you free choice, to do with life as you will. In this sense, your will for you is God's will for you.　　　　　　CG I 13

I have never set down a "right" or "wrong" a "do" or a "don't;" to do so would be to strip you completely of your greatest gift— the opportunity to do as you please, and experience the results of that.
　　To say something is "wrong" would be as much as to tell you not to do it.
　　There are those who say that I have given you free will, yet these same people claim that if you do not obey Me I will send you to hell. What kind of free will is that?　　　　CG I 39

Moses is said to have received the Ten Commandments from God in the form of a burning bush. By themselves they are a pretty good foundation to form a life around. Then, not satisfied with that, he became, *The law giver*. Making laws that said "Thou shalt not" do everything from not wearing red to not expressing a love you might have for another of the same sex. "Thou shalt not" became the rule.

Jesus of Nazareth preached love, kindness and forgiveness among other things. Then; his work finished, he died. Saul, who became Paul, became mad with power and made even more "Thou shalt

God is out

nots," making people believe that he was continuing the work of Rabbi Jesus. This does not make sense because it is the opposite of what Jesus taught. Todays "Christian" churches seldom preach the teachings of the Christ, what they teach is the writings of Paul. They should then be called, Paulists or Paulines, not Christians.

MF/BB

Life itself is a rhythm. It is a wave, a vibration, a pulsation at the very heart of All That Is. CG I 32

As stated in *Death*, vibrations or pulsations imply the necessity of an opposite, in this case it represents right vs wrong. MF/BB

You [have created] in your imaginations a power equal to God... the being you call, "Devil." You have even imagined a God at war with this being, thinking God solves problems the way you do. CG I 14,15

You are living your life the way you are living your life, and I have no preference in the matter. I do not care what you do, and that is hard for you to hear. It is this dichotomy—not caring about the process, but caring deeply about the result that comes close to describing the dichotomy [that is] God.

God does not care about the outcome, not the ultimate outcome. This is because the ultimate outcome is assured. God is the observer, not the Creator. It is not God's function to create, or un-create the circumstances or conditions of your life. CG I 13

All of life exists as a tool of your own creation, and all of its events merely present themselves as opportunities for you to decide and be, who you [really] are. CG I 32

If you want to feel bad, feel bad. But judge not, and neither condemn, for you know not why a thing occurs, nor to what end.
CG I 38

Judge not, then, the karmic path walked by another. Envy not success, Pity not failure, for you know not what is success or failure in [that] soul's reckoning. CG I 33

Do not condemn, therefore, all that you would call bad in the world. Rather, ask yourself, what about this have you judged bad, and what, if anything, you wish to do to change it.

We despise in others the faults that we see in ourselves. MF/BB

There [is] no 'should' or 'shouldn't' in God's world. Do what you want to do. Do what reflects you, what re-presents you as a grander vision of your Self. CG I 37

The greatest and most powerful thing you can do is simply to be that which you really are without judgement. MF/BB

Yet, bless *all*—for all is the creation of God through *life living*, and that is the highest creation. And [know] you this: that which you condemn will condemn you and that which you judge, you will one day become. CG I 38

Inquire within rather than without, asking: "What part of my self do I wish to experience now in the face of this calamity: What part of [my] being do I choose to call forth?" CG I 32

Seek to change those things—or support others who are changing those things which no longer reflect your highest sense of who you are. CG I 38

Judgment is often based upon previous experience. Your idea about a thing derives from a prior idea about that thing. Your prior idea results from a still prior idea—and that idea from another, and so forth. CG I 38

We are all different, in the end if you do the best that you can with what you have, it is enough. Shine with your own light, that is what you came here for. MF/BB

Nothing is painful in and of itself; pain is a result of wrong thought; an error in thinking. Pain results from a judgment you have made about a thing. Remove the judgment and the pain disappears. CG I 37

There is no such thing as karmic debt. A debt is something that must or should be repaid. You are not obligated to do anything. Still, there are certain things that you want to do [or] choose to experience. And some of these choices hinge on the desire for them [that] has been created by what you have experienced before. CG I 204

There is no judgment in what you call the afterlife. You will not even be allowed to judge yourself for you would surely give yourself a low score, given how judgmental and unforgiving you are with yourself in this life. CG I 183

Nonetheless, while there will be no judgment in the afterlife, there will be opportunity to look again at all you have thought, said and done here, and to decide if that is what you would choose again, based on who you say you are and who you want to be. CG I 183

You will have the opportunity to review again this, your present life, without pain or fear of judgment, for the purpose of deciding how you feel about your experience here, and where you want to go from there. CG I 183

There is a hell, but it is not what you think. It is the experience of the worst possible outcome of your choices, decisions, and creations. It is the pain you suffer through wrong thinking. Yet even the term "wrong thinking" is a misnomer, because there is no such thing as that which is wrong. CG I 40

Hell does not exist as this place you have fantasized, where you burn in some everlasting fire, or exist in some state of everlasting torment. What purpose could God have in that? I tell you there is no such experience after death as you have constructed in your fear based theologies. Yet there is an experience of the soul so unhappy, so incomplete, so less than whole, so separated from God's greatest joy, that to your soul this would be hell. [You are not sent there], you, yourself, create the experience whenever you deny your self—whenever you reject who and what you really are.
CG 1 41

Hell and heaven are what you have taught by religions which are based on keeping people as members of their faith; and of course paying tithes. Religions were formed for this purpose and they use fear, and have used fear for ages, consciously or unconsciously, to keep their members in line.

Your thinking is limited by the three dimensional world where you exist. As you learn more, your thinking will indeed change, and so will your circumstances.

You are like a cell within the body of All That Is,

Are you a cancer cell or a healthy one?

All that Is does not want to punish you for past "sins",
it is enough that you to realize that the hurt you have cause others (and yourself) is the pain of you kicking yourself in the butt,
for you are certainly a part of All That Is.

There is no judgement in this.
It is enough that you quit hurting others and yourself.

Can you hear All That Is giving a sigh of relief?

MF/BB

god/God

You and your personal relationship with All That Is

Here is where most people will have to pay another price for the knowledge that follows. Again, be patient with yourself as you read.

Try to let go of the idea that God is a man on a throne or other physical image. This is a depiction that makes God In the limited image of mankind. Think of a god that is unlimited; - -
    everywhere and omnipresent.

Now think of yourself;
there is no other "You" in the universe,
    there never has been and never will be.

With nothing to compare you with,
    it stands to reason that there is no other in the universe greater,
        nor less than you.
You are the best along with the worst of that which is you.
    - - You are a singular event.

If God is all things, it must include you and your surroundings.
    God, is not complete without a You.
Everyone can say this;
    we are all like molecules within the body of God.

If you are a separate part of God, you have an impact on it too.
    Like a molecule within your own body which does the same.

We all have different outlooks on the world and its happenings,
    and most of us have differing philosophies.

Therefore there is no God/god the same for anyone because you create your own separate beingness with god that can never be duplicated.　　　　　　　　　　　　　　　　　　　　　MF/BB

You cannot be what you do not know your self to be. That is why you have been given this life, so that you might know yourself in your own experience. Then you can conceive of yourself as who you really are and create yourself as that which you want to be.
　　　　　　　　　　　　　　　　　　　　　　　　　CG I 201

The "Great veil" as it has been called is nothing more than our physical and mentally limited attachment to the three dimensional world in which we find ourselves.
　　In order to understand more, you must accept that the three dimensional world that you know is only one reality, and that many other dimensions exist as well, even though you cannot see or feel them.　　　　　　　　　　　　　　　　　　MF/BB

When you consider the question of a supreme being, you may imagine a male personality whose qualities you admire. This imagined god has therefore changed throughout your centuries, mirroring man's shifting ideas of himself.　　　　　　　SS 241

When the word "God" is spoken, each of us envision a completely different picture of what is being spoken of. Many people refer to God as "He, Him, The Man upstairs," and so forth, making that entity into a form to which they can relate;
- - a three dimensional being; and a man for the most part.

So we limit our Gods by our belief that God is a three dimensional being, just as we limit ourselves with that same conviction.

Even in this discourse we have been forced to use a masculine adjective to describe that which is called God—a limitation yet again, of language.　　　　　　　　　　　　　　　　　　MF/BB

God is out 114

Each of you has understood Me— Created Me—in your own way.
To some of you I am a man. To some of you I am a woman.
To some I am both. To some I am neither.
To some of you I am pure energy.
To some, the ultimate feeling, which you call Love.
And some of you have no idea what I am.
You simply know that I AM.
And so it is. I AM.   CG II 25

And to some, God is not at all.   MF/BB

I have no form or shape [that] you understand. I could adopt a form or shape that you could understand. But then everyone would assume that what they have seen is the one and only form and shape of God, rather than "a" form or shape of God.   CG I 9

When I come in one particular form or another, a form in which I think people can understand, people assign Me that form forevermore. And should I come in any other form to any other people, the first say I did not appear to the second, because I did not look to the second as I did to the first. You see, then, it matters not in what form or in what manner I reveal Myself. Whatever manner I choose and whatever form I take, will not be incontrovertible.   CG I 10

No one can see that which is called God the same; 'YOU' are always part of the equation. The physical senses allow you to perceive the three-dimensional world, and yet by their very nature they can inhibit the perception of other equally valid dimensions.
                                                                SS 8

Even if we stand next to one another we will not see the same thing. We cannot do this because we do not look from the same eyes, direction, nor with the same perceptions or awareness.
                                                               MF/BB

I am the Great Unseen, not what I cause Myself to be in any particular moment. In a sense, I am [that which] I am not. It is from the am-not-ness that I come, and to it I always return. CG I 9

In the most inescapable truth, He is not human in your terms at all, Nor, in your terms is He a personality. Our ideas of personality are too limited to contain the multitudinous facets of His multidimensional existence. On the other hand He is human, in that He is a portion of each individual, and within the vastness of His experience He holds an "idea-shape" of Himself as human, -- to which we can relate. He literally was made flesh to dwell among you for he forms your flesh, in that, He is responsible for the energy that gives vitality and validity to your private multidimensional self, which in turn forms your image in accordance with your own ideas. SS 246, 7

Again the word *He* demonstrates the limitations of language.
MF/BB

There are no facts that can be given that can portray with any faithfulness the attributes of All That Is. SS 247

Perhaps it would be better to say that physical reality is one form that reality takes. SS 44

God was seen as cruel and powerful when man believed that these were desirable characteristics; needed particularly in his battle for physical survival. He projected these upon his idea of a god because he envied them and feared them. The old concepts of god are relatively meaningless. Even the term, "Supreme Being," is in itself distortive, for [it] naturally projects the qualities of human nature upon it. SS 241

Again, one does not *see* God, for that again would be a three dimensional and limited vision. MF/BB

God can only be experienced, and you experience Him whether or not you realize it, through your own existence. He is not male or female however, and I use the term only for convenience's sake.
SS 247

"He," again a limitation of language. MF/BB

God is out

Shakespeare again. - "Know thyself," cannot be too strongly expressed. It is my belief that you cannot know more of anything than you know of yourself. Your mind simply cannot process anything more than what and who you yourself are.

Your personal "One-ness" is something that no one else can re-create; again, you are a one of a kind event. If you wish to know more of God, begin by uncovering more of yourself.

As stated earlier, an honest assessment of who and what you are, what you do and what you have done will help to clear the blinders from your vision so you can see yourself more clearly.
    When you can truly say, "This is me,"
      you can also say, "Everything else is not me."
        All that is "me" and all that is "not me" then, is
        All That Is.

As you influence all those about you, you also influence All That Is. So a reflection of yourself and your circumstances is mirrored outward as far as you can think. Some call this God. Another name for God is All That Is.

Thus you define yourself and everything else at the same time. What you do then is up to you.

   Like the Yin/Yang symbol, You are half and God is the other half.
                                         MF/BB

Your thought about yourself is that you are not good enough,
not wondrous enough, not sinless enough to be a part of God.
You have denied for so long who you are that you have forgotten
who you are.   CG I 75

If you knew who you are—that you are the most magnificent, the most remarkable, the most splendid being God has ever created, you would never fear. For who could reject such a wondrous magnificence? Not even God could find fault in such a being.
But you do not know who you are, and you think you are a great deal less.   CG I 16

When I was growing up as a Mormon I remember a saying:
"As man is, God once was, As God is, Man might become."
I used that saying as a guide post while I was growing up.
Oddly enough, the Mormon leadership is now trying to play that
down, saying that they believe people are not yet ready for it.
MF/BB

I AM THAT I AM, and YOU ARE THAT YOU ARE.

You cannot not be.
You can change form all you wish, but you cannot fail to 'be'.
Yet you can fail to know Who You Are, and in this failing,
experience only the half of it.   CG1 200

Think of yourself as a seed; the very best that you can offer, and
bless that which grows for it is the body of god/God.   MF/BB

Now I will tell you, there are even larger truths than this to which
you will one day become privy. For even as you are the body of
Me, I am the body of another.   CG I 197

There will always be a greater God.

It is the same when our astronomers look deeper and deeper into
outer space looking for the beginning or the end. Even looking
into areas where they see nothing they find entire galaxies there in
the nothingness; their very searching causing the greater depth.
MF/BB

I closed my eyes and grew infinite; endless as God, and on.
and in the nothingness that surrounded me,
I saw a spot, - - so small as only infinites could see.
I knew that spot was me.
And it was good.
This where my symbol was born.

God is out

As my Hippie brothers and sisters used to say,
"Peace brother, Thou art god."

Part 4

Let God now, truly say

God is out

When I was researching my archives for this book, I came upon a file called, *The God Memorandum*.

I was fairly stunned because I had never seen nor heard of it; I was just getting my first book, *Follow Your Heart* published and did not have had time to have looked for something like this at that time.
   Reading it was as if it was really a memo from God to me.
It was so powerful that I sat crying as I read. I thought perhaps I had written it in some trance or something, and prepared to write to publishers and such.

But my neighbor, Jacky, (bless her) found that it had been published in 1968 by a fellow named Og Mangino in a book called, *The greatest salesman in the world*.
   I was thrilled to find that I would not be ruining my integrity by sending those letters claiming that I had written it in some kind of trance.

But where did the file come from? This worried me for some time. Then one night as I prepared to go to bed, an urge to write came upon me. I picked up a pen and wrote;

The God Memorandum is here, because I caused it to be here.
Not the phraseology I would have used at all, but the mystery was salved.

I did find a copy of the book, bought and read it.
One difference between the original and the version in my files was that the original used the nouns Thee, Thy, Thine, etc., while mine used me, my, you, I, and such.

And so I use this file because in my mind, The Ragpickers[2] God delivered it to me for this book.   MF/BB

---

2   The God memorandum came to Og Mandino via a man calling himself, The Rag Picker.

To: YOU
From: God
9/29/2013

Take counsel. I hear your cry.
It passes through the darkness, filters through the clouds, mingles with starlight, and finds its way to my heart on the path of a sunbeam.

    I have anguished over the cry of a hare choked in the noose of a snare, a sparrow tumbled from the nest of its mother, a child thrashing helplessly in a pond, and a son shedding his blood on a cross.

I bring you relief for your sorrow for I know its cause... and its cure.
You weep for all your childhood dreams that have vanished with the years.
You weep for all your self-esteem that has been corrupted by failure.
You weep for all your potential that has been bartered for security.
You weep for all your individuality that has been trampled by mobs.
You weep for all your talent that has been wasted through misuse.

You look upon yourself with disgrace and you turn in terror from the image you see in the pool. Who is this mockery of humanity staring back at you with bloodless eyes of shame? Where is the grace of your manner, the beauty of your figure, the quickness of your movement, the clarity of your mind, the brilliance of your tongue?

    Who stole your goods? Is the thief's identity known to you as it is to me?

Once you placed your head on a pillow of grass in your father's field and looked up at a cathedral of clouds and knew that all the gold of Babylon would be yours in time. Once you read from many books and wrote on many tablets, convinced beyond any doubt that all the wisdom of Solomon would be equaled and surpassed by you and the seasons would flow into years until lo, you would reign supreme in your own garden of Eden.

Do you remember who implanted those plans and dreams and seeds of hope within you?   You cannot. The passing years have

God is out

destroyed your recollection, for they have filled your mind with fear and doubt and anxiety and remorse and hate and there is no room for joyful memories where these beasts habit.

Weep no more. I am with you... and this moment is the dividing line of your life. All that has gone before is like unto no more than that time you slept in your mother's womb.

What is past is dead. Let the dead bury the dead.
    This day you return from the living dead.
This day, like unto Elijah with the widow's son,
    I stretch myself upon you three times and you live again.
This day, like unto Elisha with the Shumamite's son
    I put my mouth upon your mouth and my eyes upon your eyes and my hands upon your hands and your flesh is warm again.
This day, like unto Jesus at the tomb of Lazarus,
    I command you to come forth and you will walk from your cave of doom to begin a new life.

This is your birthday. This is your new day of birth.
Your first life, like a play of the theater, was only a rehearsal.
This time the curtain is up. This time the world watches and waits to applaud. This time you will not fail.

Light your candles. Share your cake. Pour the wine. You have been reborn. Like a butterfly from its chrysalis you will fly, - fly as high as you wish, and neither the wasps nor dragonflies nor mantids of mankind shall obstruct your mission or your search for the true riches of life.

Feel my hand upon your head. Attend to my wisdom. Let me share with you again, the secret you heard at your birth and forgot.

You are my greatest miracle. You are the greatest miracle in the world.
Those were the first words you ever heard.
Then you cried.
They all cry.

You did not believe me then, and nothing has happened in the intervening years to correct your dis-belief. For how could you be a miracle when you consider yourself a failure at the most menial of tasks? How can you be a miracle when you have little confidence in dealing with the most trivial of responsibilities? How can you be a miracle when you are shackled by debt and lie awake in torment over whence will come tomorrow's bread?
Enough. The milk that is spilled is sour.

Yet, how many prophets, how many wise men, philosophers and messengers have I sent with word of your divinity, your potential for godliness, and the secrets of achievement?

Still I love you and am with you now, through these words, to fulfill the prophet who announced that the Lord shall set his hand again, the second time, to recover the remnant of his people.

I have set my hand again. This is the second time.
You are my remnant.

It is of no avail to ask. Haven't you known, haven't you heard, hasn't it been told to you from the beginning; haven't you understood from the foundations of the earth?

You have been told that you are a divinity in disguise, a god playing a fool. You have been told that you are a special piece of work, noble in reason, infinite in faculties, express and admirable in form and moving, like an angel in action, like a god in apprehension. You have been told that you are the salt of the earth. You were given the secret even of moving mountains, of performing the impossible.

You believed no one. You burned your map to happiness, you abandoned your claim to peace of mind, you snuffed out the candles that had been placed along your destined path of glory, and then you stumbled, lost and frightened, in the darkness of futility and self-pity, until you fell into a hell of your own creation.

Then you cried and beat your breast and cursed the luck that had befallen you. You refused to accept the consequences of your own

petty thoughts and lazy deeds and you searched for a scapegoat on which to blame your failure. How quickly you found one.
You blamed me!
You cried that your handicaps, your mediocrity, your lack of opportunity, your failures were the will of God! You were wrong!

Let us take inventory. Let us first call a roll of your handicaps.
For how can I ask you to build a new life lest you have the tools?

Are you blind? Does the sun rise and fall without your witness? No. You can see, and the hundred million receptors I have placed in your eyes enable you to enjoy the magic of a leaf, a snowflake, a pond, an eagle, a child, a cloud, a star, a rose, a rainbow and the look of love. Count one blessing.

Are you deaf? Can a baby laugh or cry without your attention? No. You can hear... and the twenty-four thousand fibers I have built in each of your ears vibrate to the wind in the trees, the tides on the rocks, the majesty of an opera, a robin's plea, children at play and the word I love you. Count another blessing.

Are you mute? Do your lips move and bring forth only spittle? No. You can speak.. as can no other of my creatures, and your words can calm the angry, uplift the despondent, goad the quitter, cheer the unhappy, warm the lonely, praise the worthy, encourage the defeated, teach the ignorant and say I love you. Count another blessing.

Are you paralyzed? Does your helpless form despoil the land? No. You can move. You are not a tree condemned to a small plot while the wind and world abuse you. You can stretch and run and dance and work, for within you I have designed five hundred muscles, two hundred bones, and seven miles of nerve fibre all synchronized by me to do your bidding. Count another blessing.

Are you unloved and unloving? Does loneliness engulf you, night and day? No. No more. For now you know love's secret, that to receive love it must be given with no thought of its return. To love for fulfillment, satisfaction, or pride is not love. Love is a gift on which no return is demanded. Now you know that to love unselfishly is its own reward. And even should love not be returned it is not lost, for love not reciprocated will flow back to you and soften and purify your heart. Count another blessing. Count twice.

Is your heart stricken? Does it leak and strain to maintain your life? No. Your heart is strong. Touch your chest and feel its rhythm, pulsating, hour after hour, day and night, thirty-six million beats each year, year after year, asleep or awake, pumping your blood through more than sixty-thousand miles of veins, arteries, and tubing... pumping more than six hundred thousand gallons each year. Man has never created such a machine. Count another blessing.

Are you diseased of skin? Do people turn in horror when you approach? No. Your skin is clear and a marvel of creation, needing only that you tend it with soap and oil and brush and care. In time all steels will tarnish and rust, but not your skin. Eventually the strongest of metals will wear, with use, but not that layer that I have constructed around you. Constantly it renews itself, old cells replaced by new, just as the old you is now replaced by the new. Count another blessing.

Are your lungs befouled? Does the breath of life struggle to enter your body? No. Your portholes to life support you even in the vilest of environments of your own making, and they labor always to filter life-giving oxygen through six hundred million pockets of folded flesh while they rid your body of gaseous wastes. Count another blessing.

Is your blood poisoned? Is it diluted with water and pus? No. Within your five quarts of blood are twenty-two trillion blood cells and within each cell are millions of molecules and within each molecule is an atom oscillating at more than ten million times each second. Each second, two million of your blood cells die to be replaced by two million more in a resurrection that has continued since your first birth. As it has always been inside, so now it is on your outside. Count another blessing.

Are you feeble of mind? Can you no longer think for yourself? No. Your brain is the most complex structure in the universe. I know. Within its three pounds are thirteen billion nerve cells, more than three times as many cells as there are people on your earth. To help you file away every perception, every sound, every taste, every smell, every action you have experienced since the day of your birth, I have implanted, within your cells, more than one thousand billion billion protein molecules. Every incident in your life is there waiting only your recall. And, to assist your brain in the control of your body I have dispersed, throughout your form, four million pain-sensitive structures, five hundred thousand touch detectors, and more than two hundred thousand temperature detectors.

Obviously there are many who will find themselves with one or more of these handicaps. To you I say that your spiritual self chose for you to experience your particular problems in order to give you an opportunity to grow. Use them then, and overcome the physical problems so that both your physical and spiritual selves can grow.
Back to God. MF/BB

No nation's gold is better protected than you.
None of your ancient wonders are greater than you.
You are my finest creation.

Within you is enough atomic energy to destroy any of the world's great cities... and rebuild it.

Are you poor? Is there no gold or silver in your purse? No. You are rich! Together we have just counted your wealth. Study the list. Count them again. Tally your assets!

Why have you betrayed yourself? Why have you cried that all the blessings of humanity were removed from you? Why did you deceive yourself that you were powerless to change your life? Are you without talent, senses, abilities, pleasures, instincts, sensations, and pride? Are you without hope? Why do you cringe in the shadows, a giant defeated, awaiting only sympathetic transport into the welcome void and dampness of hell?

You have so much. Your blessings overflow your cup and you have been unmindful of them, like a child spoiled in luxury, since I have bestowed them upon you with generosity and regularity. What rich man, old and sick, feeble and helpless, would not exchange all the gold in his vault for the blessings you have treated so lightly.

Know then the first secret to happiness and success—that you possess, even now, every blessing necessary to achieve great glory. They are your treasure, your tools with which to build, starting today,

the foundation for a new and better life.
Therefore, I say unto you, count your blessings and know that you already are my greatest creation. This is the first law you must obey in order to perform the greatest miracle in the world, the return of your humanity from living death.

And be grateful for your lessons learned in poverty. For he is not poor who has little; only he that desires much and true security lies not in the things one has but in the things one can do without.

Where are the handicaps that produced your failure? They existed only in your mind.

Count your blessings.

And the second law is like unto the first. Proclaim your rarity.

You had condemned yourself to a potter's field, and there you lay, unable to forgive your own failure, destroying yourself with self-hate, self-incrimination, and revulsion at your crimes against yourself and others.

I address you now, for three reasons. You need me. You are not one of a herd heading for destruction in a gray mass of mediocrity. And you are a great rarity. Consider a painting by Rembrandt or a bronze by Degas or a violin by Stradivarius or a play by Shakespeare. They have great value for two reasons: their creators were masters and they are few in number. Yet there are more than one of each of these.

On that reasoning you are the most valuable treasure on the face of the earth, for you know who created you and their is only one of you. Never, until the end of time, will their be another such as you. You have shown no knowledge or appreciation of your uniqueness. Yet, you are the rarest thing in the world.

From your father, in his moment of supreme love, flowed countless seeds of love, more than four hundred million in number. All of them, as they swam within your mother, gave up the ghost and died.

All except one! You.
You alone preserved within the loving warmth of your mother's body, searching for your other half, a single cell from your mother so small that more than two million would be necessary to fill an acorn shell. Yet, despite impossible odds, in that vast ocean of darkness and disaster, you persevered, found that infinitesimal cell, joined with it, and began a new life. Your life! You arrived, bringing with you, as does every child, the message that I was not yet discouraged of man.

Two cells now united in a miracle. Two cells, each containing twenty-three chromosomes and within each chromosome hundreds of genes, which would govern every characteristic about you, from the color of your eyes to the charm of your manner, to the size of your brain.

With the combinations at my command, beginning with that single sperm from your fathers four hundred million, through the hundreds of genes in each of the chromosomes from your mother and father, I could have created three hundred thousand billion humans, each different from the other. But who did I bring forth? You! One of a kind; rarest of the rare. A priceless treasure, possessed of qualities in mind and speech and movement and appearance and actions as no other who has ever lived lives or shall live.

Why have you valued yourself in pennies when you are worth a king's ransom? Why did you listen to those who demeaned you.. and far worse, why did you believe them?

Take counsel. No longer hide your rarity in the dark.
Bring it forth. Show the world.

Strive not to walk as your brother walks, nor talk as your leader talks, nor labor as do the mediocre. Never do as another.
Never imitate. For how do you know that you may not imitate evil; and he who imitates evil always goes beyond the example set,
while he who imitates what is good always falls short. Imitate no one. Be yourself. Show your rarity to the world and they will shower you with gold.

This then is the second law.
Proclaim your rarity.

And now you have received two laws.
Count your blessings! Proclaim your rarity!
You have no handicaps. You are not mediocre.

What of your next complaint? Opportunity never seeks you?
Take counsel and it shall come to pass, for now I give you the law of success in every venture.

Many centuries ago this law was given to your forefathers from a mountain top. Some heeded the law and lo, their life was filled with the fruit of happiness, accomplishment, gold and peace of mind. Most listened not, for they sought magic means, devious routes, or waited for the devil called luck to deliver to them the riches of life. They waited in vain.... Just as you waited, and then they wept, as you wept, blaming their lack of fortune on my will.

The law is simple. Young or old, pauper or king, white or black, male or female... all can use the secret to their advantage; for of all the rules and speeches and scriptures of success and how to attain it, only one method has never failed... whomsoever shall compel ye to go with him one mile... go with him two.

This then is the third law... the secret that will produce riches and acclaim beyond your dreams.

Go another mile!

The only certain means of success is to render more and better service than is expected of you, no matter what your task may be. This is a habit followed by all successful people since the beginning of time. Therefore I say the surest way to doom yourself to mediocrity is to perform only the work for which you are paid.

Think now you are being cheated if you deliver more than the silver you receive. For there is a pendulum to all life and the sweat you deliver, if not rewarded today, will swing back tomorrow, tenfold.

God is out

The mediocre never goes another mile, for why should he cheat himself, he thinks. But you are not mediocre. To go another mile is a privilege you must appropriate by your own initiative. You cannot, you must not avoid it. Neglect it, do only as little as the others, and the responsibility for your failure is yours alone.

You can no more render service without receiving just compensation than you can withhold the rendering of it without suffering the loss of reward. Cause and effect, means and ends, seed and fruit, these cannot be separated. The effect already blooms in the cause, the end pre-exists in the means, and the fruit is always in the seed. Go another mile.

Concern yourself not, should you serve and ungrateful master. Serve him more. And instead of him, let it be me who is in your debt, for then you will know that every minute, every stroke of extra service will be repaid. And worry not, should your reward not come soon. For the longer payment is withheld, the better for you... and compound interest on compound interest is the law's greatest benefit.

You cannot command success, you can only deserve it... and now you know the great secret necessary in order to merit its rare reward.

Go another mile!

Where is this field whence you cried there was no opportunity? Look! Look around you. See, where only yesterday you wallowed on the refuse of self-pity, you now walk tall on a carpet of gold. Nothing has changed... except you, but you are everything.

You are my greatest miracle.
You are the greatest miracle in the world.

And now the laws of happiness and success are three.
Count your blessings! Proclaim your rarity! Go another mile!

Be patient with your progress. To count your blessings with gratitude, to proclaim your rarity with pride, to go an extra mile and then another, these acts are not accomplished in the blinking of an eye. Yet that which you acquire with most difficulty you retain the longest; as those who have earned a fortune are more careful of it than those by whom it was inherited. And fear not as you enter your new life. Every noble acquisition is attended with its risks. He who fears to encounter the one must not expect to obtain the other. Now you know you are a miracle. And there is no fear in a miracle.

Be proud. You are not the momentary whim of a careless creator experimenting in the laboratory of a life. You are not a slave of forces that you cannot comprehend. You are a free manifestation of no force but mine, of no love but mine. You were made with a purpose.

Feel my hand. Hear my words.
    You need me... and I need you.

We have a world to rebuild.. and if it requireth a miracle what is that to us? We are both miracles and now we have each other.

Never have I lost faith in you since that day when I first spun you from a giant wave and tossed you helplessly on the sands. As you measure time that was more than five hundred million years ago.
There were many models, many shapes, many sizes, before I reached perfection in you more than thirty thousand years ago. I have made no further effort to improve on you in all these years.
For how could one improve on a miracle? You were a marvel to behold and I was pleased. I gave you this world and dominion over it. Then, to enable you to reach your full potential I placed my hand upon you once more, and endowed you with powers unknown to any other creature in the universe, even unto this day.

I gave you the power to think.
I gave you the power to love.
I gave you the power to will.
I gave you the power to laugh.
I gave you the power to imagine.
I gave you the power to create.
I gave you the power to plan.

I gave you the power to speak.
I gave you the power to pray.

My pride in you knew no bounds. You were my ultimate creation, my greatest miracle: A complete living being. One who can adjust to any climate, any hardship, any challenge. One who can manage his own destiny without any interference from me. One who can translate a sensation of perception, not by instinct, but by thought and deliberation into whatever action is best for himself and all humanity.

Thus we come to the forth law of success and happiness... for I gave you one more power, a power so great that not even my angels posses it.

I gave you the power to choose.

With this gift I placed you even above my angels... for angels are not free to choose sin. I gave you complete control over your destiny.
I told you to determine, for yourself, your own nature in accordance with your own free will. Neither heavenly nor earthly in nature, you were free to fashion yourself in whatever form you preferred.
You had the power to choose to degenerate into the lowest forms of life, but you also had the power, out of your soul's judgement, to be reborn into the higher forms, which are divine.

I have never withdrawn that great power, the power to choose.
What have you done with this tremendous force? Look at yourself. Think of the choices you have made in your life and recall, now, those bitter moments when you would fall to your knees if only you had the opportunity to choose again.

What is past is past... and now you know the forth, great law of happiness and success...
Use wisely, your power of choice.

Choose to love.. rather than hate.
Choose to laugh.. rather than cry.
Choose to create.. rather than destroy.

Choose to persevere.. rather than quit.
Choose to praise.. rather than gossip.
Choose to heal.. rather than wound.
Choose to give.. rather than steal.
Choose to act.. rather than procrastinate.
Choose to grow.. rather than rot.
Choose to pray.. rather than curse.
Choose to live.. rather than die.

Now you know that your misfortunes were not my will, for all power was vested in you, and the accumulation of deeds and thoughts which placed you on the refuse of humanity were your doing, not mine. My gifts of power were too large for your small nature. Now you have grown tall and wise and the fruits of the land will be yours.

You are more than a human being, you are a human becoming.
You are capable of great wonders. Your potential is unlimited. Who else, among my creatures, has mastered fire? Who else, among my creatures, has conquered gravity, has pierced the heavens, has conquered disease and pestilence and drought?

Never demean yourself again!
Never settle for the crumbs of life!
Never hide your talents, from this day hence!

Remember the child who says, "When I am a big boy." But what is that? For the big boy says, "When I grow up." And when grown up, he says, "When I am wed." The thought then changes to "When I retire." And then, retirement comes, and he looks back over the landscape traversed; a cold wind sweeps over it and somehow he has missed it all and it is gone.

Enjoy this day, today.. and tomorrow, tomorrow.
You have performed the greatest miracle in the world.
You have returned from a living death.

You will feel self-pity no more and each new day will be a challenge and a joy.

God is out

You have been born again... but just as before, you can choose failure and despair or success and happiness. The choice is yours. The choice is exclusively yours. I can only watch, as before... in pride ... or sorrow.

Remember, then, the four laws of happiness and success.

Count your blessings.
Proclaim your rarity.
Go another mile.
Use wisely your power of choice.

And one more, to fulfill the other four.

Do all things with love, love for yourself, love for all others and love for me.
Wipe away your tears. Reach out, grasp my hand, and stand straight. Let me cut the grave cloths that have bound you. This day you have been notified.

You are the greatest miracle in the world.

Given to Og Mandino by Simon Potter and Lazaras - 1972
and to Michael Fleming/Brahmacharya Baba by the author - 9/29/2013

MF/BB

The New Gospel for the Age of Ages

What is the secret to lasting peace?
Throughout the ages I have given you the answer.
Throughout the ages, I have brought you this wisdom,
a thousand times in a thousand ways.
Yet you have not listened.

Now I declare it here, in language so plain that you can never
again ignore it, but will understand it completely, and internalize
it so deeply, that you hereafter and forevermore reject any
suggestion that one group of you is somehow better than another
group of you.

> Again I say put an End to Better.
> For this is The New Gospel:

There Is no master race. There is no greatest nation.
There is no one true religion.
There is no inherently perfect philosophy.
There is no always right political party, morally supreme
economic system,
or one and only way to Heaven.

Erase these ideas from your memory.
Eliminate them from your experience.
Eradicate them from you your culture.
For these are thoughts of division and separation,
and you have killed each other over these thoughts. .

Only the truth I give you here will save now:

WE ARE ALL ONE.

Carry this message far and wide,
across oceans and over continents,
around the corner and around the world.   FG 58,9

Just some of the pasted pages
that went into this work.

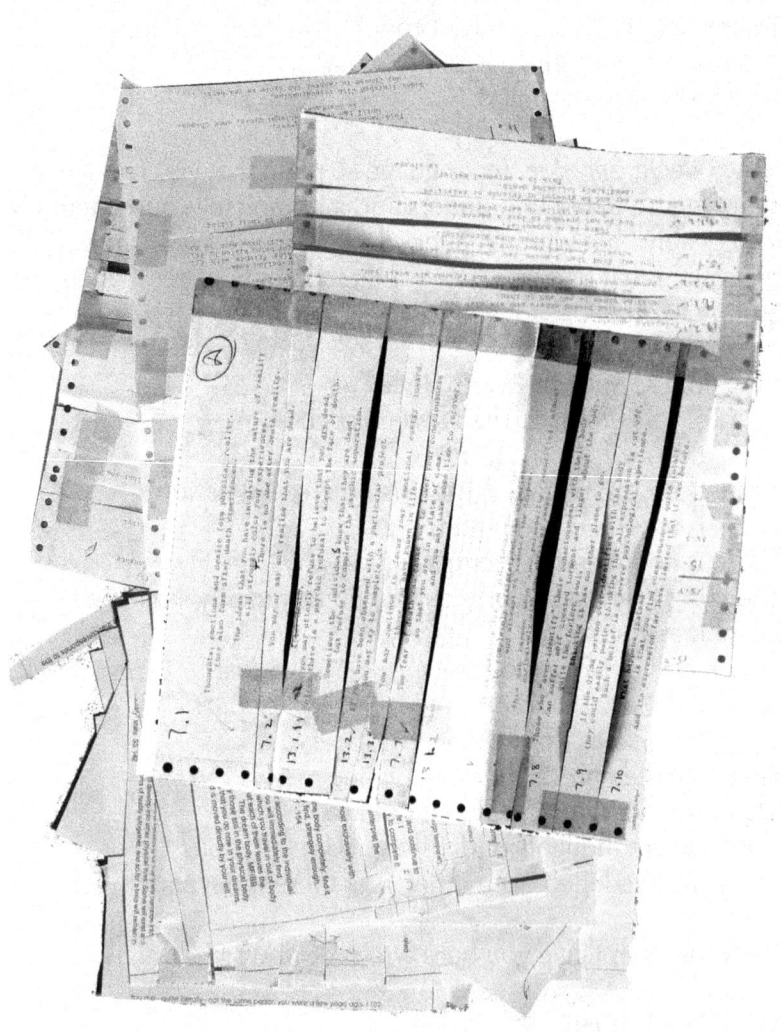

MF/BB

This is the Age of Ages. What is the Age of Ages?

"It is said that a new force entered the world in 1959, and it is interesting to note that the Great Pyramid prophecies ended on November, 1959 at which time mankind symbolically passed from the King's Chamber into The Great Hall of Union."
(Word of One, received by Rosalind Sharpe and John Cook, 1975)

Many other things mark this time:

The end of the century - 100 years.
The end of the Millennium - 1,000 years.
The end of the age of Pisces and the beginning of the Age of Aquarius - about 2,160 years.
The end of the fifth and last cycle of the Mayan calendar - about 5,126 years
The end of the five sun cycles of the Mayan calendar - 25,625 years.
The galactic alignment of our sun with the equator of the Milky Way galaxy on 12/21/2012 - about 26,000 years; around the same time as the ending of the five cycles of the Mayan calendar.

Thus 12/21/12 is very significant in transcendent teaching, for the Mayan depiction of this date is 13.0.0.0.0 - this number is both the ending and the beginning number - at that time the Mayans believed we begin anew.

With all of these alignments, plus mankind's evolution, we all stand now at the beginning of a new age with its own understandings.

If ever there is to be an "Age of Ages," this is it.
    Now is the time foretold.

It is also said that at this time, power will pass from male confrontational energy to the more loving female energy.
Let us hope that this is true.   MF/BB

Bibliography

Parts 3 and 4 of this book
are collections transcribed, edited and arranged from
the following books combined with writings
by Michael Fleming/Brahmacharya Baba

Part 3
Conversations with God Book 1 1995 (CG I)
Conversations with God book 2 1997 (CG II)

Friendship with God 1999 (FG)
Delivered through Neale Donald Walsch

Seth Speaks 1972 (SS)
Delivered though Jane Roberts

The word of ONE 1975 (ONE)
Delivered through John Cooke and Rosalind Sharpe

Fantz Fanon – quoted material.

Part 4
Memorandum from God
From *The Greatest Miracle in the World* 1973
Delivered to Og Mandino
and revealed to me 9/29/2013

The New Gospel
From *Friendship with God* 1999
Delivered though Neale Donald Walsch